BUTTERFIELD 8
JOHN O'HARA

THE HAT ON THE BED
A COLLECTION
OF 24 NEW
STORIES BY
JOHN
O'HARA
A RANDOM HOUSE BOOK

en North
rederick
hn O'Hara

by JOHN O'HARA
author of APPOINTMENT IN SAMARRA

The
DOCTOR'S SON
and other stories

RAGE
to LIVE
A NOVEL BY
JOHN O'HARA

JOHN O'HARA

A NOVEL
BY JOHN O'HARA
From the Terrace
A RANDOM HOUSE BOOK

THE
Farmers Hotel
A NOVEL BY John O'Hara

PAL JOEY
by John O'Hara

WAITING
FOR
WINTER
OLLECTION
OHN
O'HARA

THE
BIG
LAUGH
a novel by
JOHN
O'HARA

JOHN
Files on
Parade
O'HARA

John O'Hara
SWEET
AND
SOUR

THE
LOCKWOOD
CONCERN
A NOVEL BY
JOHN
O'HARA
A RANDOM HOUSE BOOK

JOHN
O'HARA
Lovey Childs:
A PHILADELPHIAN'S STORY

APPOINTMENT
IN SAMARRA
by
JOHN
O'HARA

O'Hara

JOHN O'HARA: A CHECKLIST

lot 12 5c

Compiled by
MATTHEW J. BRUCCOLI

With a previously unpublished speech by
JOHN O'HARA

Random House New York

John O'Hara:
A Checklist

TO CHARLES MANN

FIRST PRINTING

Library of Congress Cataloging in Publication Data
Bruccoli, Matthew Joseph, 1931–
    John O'Hara; a checklist.
    1. O'Hara, John, 1905–1970—Bibliography.
I. O'Hara, John, 1905–1970. II. Title.
Z8642.32.B7   016.813'5'2   72–2693
ISBN 0–394–46991–7

Manufactured in the United States of America
by Kingsport Press, Inc., Kingsport, Tennessee.

INTRODUCTION

THIS CHECKLIST OF JOHN O'HARA should be regarded as a working bibliography, since it is the first attempt to compile a comprehensive list of his published work.

John O'Hara published more words than any other major American writer of the century, but he kept no record—not even scrapbooks—of his work. I am confident that I have located all of his important writings; but most of O'Hara's journalism is still unidentified—he did not receive a by-line on some of the publications he worked for (*Pottsville Journal, Tamaqua Courier, Time, Pittsburgh Bulletin Index*). The policy here for journalism is to list feature articles and omit straight reporting.

The rationale for the first section of this checklist—Books by John O'Hara—is to provide a description of the first printing of the first edition and then to list all reprints of all editions in English. The terms *printing* (or *reprinting*) and *edition* are used carefully. An *edition* includes all the separate printings made from a single setting of type. A *printing* consists of the copies made at one time (i.e., from one press run) of a particular edition. Under each title the arabic numbers indicate new editions; within each edition the letters designate each new publisher. For *Appointment in Samarra* there are 11 editions. Thus, I-1F indicates the 1953 Modern Library reprinting of *Appointment in Samarra* from the 1934 Harcourt, Brace first-edition plates. This Modern Library publication went through nine printings by 1964. One of the functions of a bibliography is to provide information about the development of an author's career in terms of the distribution of his work, and in the case of John O'Hara the information is not fully usable without a record of his paperback appearances.

Dates in brackets are not on the title pages. For the paperbacks the serial number is given for the first printing only; if the number was altered in a subsequent printing, this fact is not noted. Asterisks indicate entries the compiler has not seen. The following categories of material have been omitted: mimeographed acting scripts of plays, mimeographed motion-picture scripts, book-dealer catalogues that quote O'Hara letters or inscriptions (with one exception included in the Letters section).

Any bibliographical project is a collaboration. I therefore gratefully acknowledge the help of my collaborators: Charles Mann, Pennsylvania State University Libraries (the repository for John O'Hara's papers) ; Frederick A. and H. Nancy Hetzel, the *Tamaqua Courier;* Alexander Clark, Princeton University Library; Albert Erskine, Suzanne Beves, and James Wilcox, Random House; Anthony Rota; the superb staff of the British Museum; Mrs. Mary Goolsby, University of South Carolina Library; Mrs. Janet Abrahamsen; and Dr. Jennifer Atkinson. My special debt, as always, is to C. E. F. Clark, Jr.

University of South Carolina
11 April 1972

CONTENTS

FOYLE'S LUNCHEON
3 May '67

IN SPITE OF THE FACT that it is almost thirty years since I first came to London, and in spite of the fact that London is one of my favorite cities, this is my debut as a public speaker in your town. On my earliest visits, while I was still a young man, I gave what might be called a series of private lectures in such cultural institutions as the Ivy restaurant, the Savoy Grill, the 400 Club, Quaglino's, l'Apéritif, the Savage Club, and various locals in S.W.3. My comments on your manners and customs were not always well received. Perhaps I was over-conscientious in my endeavors to be fair. That is to say, to be just as fair to the English as countless Englishmen since Mr. Dickens had been to my country. As you know, Mr. Dickens and many other gentlemen, less talented but equally observant, did not fail to notice certain imperfections in my homeland. I therefore took it upon myself to achieve a fair balance. But there is no such thing as a fair balance in matters of this kind, and thirty years ago no one remembered that Dickens and all the others had had their say about the United States. Consequently my informal lectures in the Savoy Grill and the 400 Club were treated with disdain, as though they were the intemperate utterances of a youngish man who had a great deal to learn about England and as much to learn about his capacity for whiskey.

Regrettably I have learned the hard way that my capacity for whiskey is nil. Rather less regrettably I have learned a little more about England. Or let me say, immodestly, that I have learned a little more about the human race, in which I gladly include the English.

Whether I like it or not—and sometimes I don't—I have been tagged with the epithet, social historian. When it is used in complimentary fashion, the label is a dangerous one because an author so described may begin to think of himself as a social historian and fall into the habit of writing like one. It is probably safe to say that every writer of fiction was a social historian. We can go further and suggest that every great writer of fiction was a great social historian. But he was first of all and always an artist, and what more could he ask? I don't know the origin of the term, but I am inclined to suspect that it was invented by a critic who believed that it was more profoundly complimentary to call an author a social historian than an artist. At the risk of being judged unfair— a risk I am willing to take in the case of critics—I shall go on suspecting that it was a critic who decided that Dickens or Zola or Balzac could be made to seem more important by calling them social historians. Since I want you to feel that I am an important *something,* and as I am much too modest to insist that I am an important artist, I address you today as a social historian. You should get home in time for tea, stimulated to the point of exhaustion by the things I have told you. If tea does not revive you, I urge you to knock back a few whiskies, and I wish I could join you.

As a social historian it becomes my duty to give you hell for the things that have been happening in your country, and you are supposed to sit here and politely take it. But I don't see how I can give you hell without—in all fairness— placing some of the blame on my own country. As a matter of fact, many of the things that I don't like about England today are un-English, and when I come here from time to time and find so much that is un-English, I am bitterly disappointed. Some of you may have seen what has happened to Times Square, in New York City, and to Forty-second Street. The honky-tonk atmosphere has taken the place of the old-time glamor, and while there is plenty of excitement in that area, it is the kind of excitement that makes me stay away from our Broadway and hasten to the peace and quiet of yours. As I have said on other occasions, when the English copy the

Americans they copy the wrong things. I was distressed some years ago to discover that the works of Damon Runyon were enjoying a vogue in England, and that there was a cult of Runyonados who affected Runyonesque speech in the entirely erroneous belief that there were people who talked that way. The thing I most disliked about Runyon's writing was its fundamental dishonesty. I knew Runyon and I knew the people he had in mind when he was writing. They were no damn good. They were thieves and chiselers, and if any of them had had a heart of gold it would have been cut out of them by their companions. The sad thing is that Runyon could have been a social historian; no one knew the gangsters and the gamblers and the pimps and prostitutes better than he, and he could write. But he never told the truth about them. He gave them a sort of raffish innocence that made them as acceptable as the characters in P. G. Wodehouse. Come to think of it, Wodehouse invented one Runyonesque character. I refer to the pig, but it was a well-bred pig.

I suppose that there have been thousands of Americans who lived and died without ever knowing that the English countryside was not inhabited by murderers and murder victims. You must realize that the only English books many of my countrymen have read were mystery novels, and that a rather gory picture was presented of the goings-on in the stately homes. The hacks who wrote your mystery novels were as much to blame for this somewhat inaccurate picture of rural England as Runyon for his picture of urban America, but possibly because Runyon wrote more effectively he did the greater harm. At least I never heard of an American cult that tried to talk like Lord Peter Wimsey. We do have in the United States an organization called the Baker Street Irregulars, who put on deerstalkers and read self-consciously scholarly papers on the works of Sir Arthur Conan Doyle, but Sir Arthur is entitled to serious consideration as artist and social historian, if only because he can transport you back to the England of his time, the sights and sounds and smells of

London and the countryside, so economically and so truly. The plots of Sir Arthur's stories are wasted on me; I read and reread them to spend a few hours in a place and a time that existed before I was born. It is a time and a place that I sometimes wish I could return to. Failing that, I come to the United Kingdom once in a while and try to ignore what I do not wish to see. You will agree, however, that it becomes increasingly difficult to avoid the sight of the strange young creatures who call attention to themselves with their odd attire, while at the same time hiding their identity behind growths of hair. This, by the way, is one of the mysteries of present-day youth, this business of dressing eccentrically to achieve distinction, and at the same time encouraging a hirsute bush that automatically robs them of recognition. It is true that Lady Godiva covered as much as she could with her long tresses, but today's young people are hardly motivated by the same high principles. It occurs to me that if Lady Godiva were to ride bareback in the Haymarket at noon tomorrow, she would be safe from the peeping Toms. The peeping Toms can now sit comfortably in a strip tease joint in no danger from Lady Godiva's charger. In our country we have been having a vogue of restaurants with topless waitresses. Over here I suppose they would be known as milk bars.

Enough of that. I am more or less at peace with the Lord Chamberlain at the moment, and I'd like to keep it that way.

When I was invited to make an appearance here, it was suggested to Mr. Graham Watson, who so capably handles my literary affairs in the U. K., that my discourse might be on the subject of literary awards and their effect on authors. I have been wondering about that. Mr. Watson also represents Mr. John Steinbeck, and I suspect that someone must be under the impression that all of Mr. Watson's clients are winners of the Nobel Prize. Not so. I confess that there was a time when I thought I had a chance of going to Stockholm to get the medal and the 15,000 guineas or whatever it is in cash. I even practiced saying "Thank You" in Swedish. "Tack så mycket," one says, and they reply, "Var so god." It was not just an idle dream. A renowned winner of the Nobel who lived in London passed the word on to an English friend of mine that I had been up three times or maybe it was four. I was so sure that my turn would come that I promised myself a Rolls-Royce if I won. Well, I have the Rolls-Royce, but I gave it to myself as a consolation prize two years ago when it became certain that the Swedes were not even going to give me a Volvo.

I have grown so fond of my Rolls that if the Swedish Academy were to offer me the Nobel, conditionally on my giving up my Rolls, I would be compelled to say, "Tack så mycket, but no, tacks." An author with such a frivolous attitude is probably not Nobel Prize material anyway. Hemingway never bought a Rolls. Faulkner never bought a Rolls. Pearl S. Buck never bought a Rolls. Sinclair Lewis never bought a Rolls. Steinbeck never bought a Rolls. Tom Eliot never bought a Rolls. And I would hazard a guess that none of those rather obscure authors whom the Swedish Academy likes to surprise us with will be found on the rolls of Rolls-Owners. You must, you *must* be serious. You must be deadly serious, as deadly serious, let us say, as dynamite. If you are likewise obscure, in both meanings of the word, it is so much the better. The somewhat less than unanimous approval of the award to Steinbeck was caused, I believe, by the fact that whatever else he may or may not be, Steinbeck is not obscure. At the time of the award to Steinbeck one critic complained that Steinbeck and I were lightweights. Immediately the question arises, "Then what is a heavyweight?" I suggest that the answer to that is to be found in the unreadability of so many writers who never learned what writing is for. Writing is for reading, as music is for hearing and painting is for seeing. Writing for reading is an even more serious obligation to its creator than music for hearing is to the composer or painting for seeing is to the artist. Music, of course, has an advantage that writing and painting lack. Strike a C-chord and you get the attention of every man, woman, or child, regardless of their intellectual capacity. A painting, a drawing, has an almost equally elemental, fundamental appeal. But the art of writing presupposes the existence of a reader with a trained mind, trained at least to the degree that the printed words will have meaning. You and I do not open a volume in Sanskrit or Japanese or even the Cyrillic and make any sense out of the characters. It is usually forgotten, in highbrow discussions of the various arts, that writing is the only art that demands special training on the part of everyone who takes even the slightest interest in the form. H. L. Mencken once declared that no one can appreciate music who has not learned to read the bass clef. I disagree. No one loves music more than I do, and I have long since forgotten how to read the bass clef. I listen to some music every day of my life. As for the graphic arts, all you need is an eye or two. You look, you are attracted or repelled or both. But to appreciate writing you first have had to learn to read.

Now of course I am not going to argue that the woman who reads every word of *News of the World* is more of an intellectual than the woman who reads nothing at all but spends her leisure hours in the Albert Hall or the British Museum. But let us strike a medium. As Noel Coward did not say in *Blithe Spirit,* some mediums should be struck regularly, like gongs. Let us invent an average person, let us call her Mrs. Tommy Atkins. Let us say that our Mrs. Atkins is an educated person, educated up to the university level. A literate person. Able to read. And let us say that our Mrs. Atkins does read, not only the *News of the World,* but occasionally the novels of Mr. John Braine, Mr. Graham Greene, Mr. John Steinbeck, and other authors who have taken pains to be readable. I mention only a few, but a noteworthy few of the authors who, different though they may be, one from another, do have in common this conscientious approach to their work. Our Mrs. Atkins may turn away from one of these authors because she does not care for his people, or because she does not care to be preached to, however subtly. But she does not turn away because of these authors' unreadability. I cannot make that point too often. I make it as often as I can because the intellectual community, the highbrow critics, have got into the habit of dismissing readability as a small virtue and very nearly a fault. It is not hard to see why. I read these critics and they are unreadable in 700 words, but that does not keep them from being disrespectful to a novel of 700 pages. By the way, you must not expect modesty from me. I am just as aware as anyone else that my books have sold something like 15 million copies, and I could not have attained that circulation if I had not been readable. Dear Mrs. Atkins, may her tribe increase. Since 1934 I have published more than twenty-five books—novels, novellas, and collections of short stories. One of the very nicest things about you English is your loyalty to your entertainers, your actors and actresses and variety artists. To some extent this devotion is matched by your willingness to do the same for authors. But Mrs. Atkins does not go on reading an author who ceases to be readable, and for this no one is to blame but the author. Let an author become careless or cocky or simply written out, and Mrs. Atkins will abandon him. I am very happy to say that she has not abandoned me. After thirty-three years, beginning with a best-seller, and often in spite of Mr. Connolly's enemies of promise, I still manage to find my books on the current best-seller lists. And do you know why? Because I give them what *I* want. Not what *they* want. The author who believes he is going to *give them what they want* is making a great, great mistake, for the truth is that they don't know what they want. And for an author to attempt to anticipate what they want is an act of dishonesty. It may be all very well for a Gracie Fields to come out once again and once again to sing the "Biggest Aspidistra in the World," and for Louis Armstrong to sing "Hello, Dolly!" for the ten thousandth time. But the casualty list of authors who repeated themselves is long and dismal. They paid for their dishonesty with the loss of Mrs. Atkins's loyalty.

We're getting somewhere. I am sneaking up on a point, and that point is that the authors who love their work and are conscientious about it are the first to know when carelessness or cockiness or creative sterility sets in. The distractions and diversions can be temporary or totally destructive, and they can be anything from booze to women to greed to too much praise. Between the invasion of Poland and the Japanese surrender I found that I could not write anything longer than a short story. You might say that it took a world war to keep me away from my typewriter. You might also say that when I got back to my typewriter I went to work with a vengeance—a vengeance, possibly, on those critics who said I was written out. Well, the revenge has been sweet, not because I have demolished my critics, but because I have been doing what I want to do and to my satisfaction doing it better than I had ever done it before.

In one sense I could call myself a war profiteer—in the sense that I profited by the long absence from the typewriter, during which I built up a reserve of impatience and frustration that finally, when I got back to the typewriter, converted itself into energy. If you are the sort of egocentric, sensitive individual who chooses writing for his life work, wartime is an emotional experience like no other. No one escapes the dreariness and the drama, and when you have been previously conditioned by your work to see and hear and share every detail of human behavior, there is not a single minute that does not provide you with—and here comes that awful word—material. At such a time you are rather like a man locked inside the Bank of England, surrounded by cash but unable to spend a penny. But when the opportunity came, when peace of a sort was restored in the world and I no longer felt that it was my duty to second-guess the Prime Minister and the President of the United States, I found that my resources were practically unlimited. I am not exaggerating when I say that I could keep busy for the next ten years. I know, for instance, what my publishing schedule will be in 1969. The one thing

I dislike about getting older is that it is no longer physically possible for me to stay at the typewriter for seven or eight hours at a stretch, which I have been known to do many times. After four hours at my desk I find that when I try to raise my 14 stone deadweight, my legs buckle under me. If that were not so, I could predict with accuracy how many books I shall have published between now and 1975, when I hope to have the original Mrs. Atkins's granddaughter among my readers.

I touch upon the physical resources only lightly, since it is perfectly obvious that after sixty we can all expect to slow down a bit, and I am sixty-two. Last year I had to become reconciled to the fact that even such an undemanding pastime as golf was taking it out of me. My physician told me that I ought to take more exercise, but my surgeon told me that my bad back was inoperable. I had been playing golf for almost fifty years, and I could have won the British Open IF I had only worked as hard on my golf as I do on my writing. The same with tennis. You'd have seen me out there on the center court at Wimbledon, saying, "Hello, Queen," but for the fact that when I was four years old I learned to read. By the way, it was around that time that I first contracted a mild case of Anglophilia which has been with me all my life. An aunt of mine—an American, of course—used to give me every Christmas a copy of THIS YEAR'S BOOK FOR BOYS. She was not of Irish descent, and I sometimes wonder why she chose that Edwardian volume of insidious British propaganda. But I loved it, although I never was won over to cricket. However, I was never really won over to baseball either. Reading, and then writing, never had to win me over. I took to reading, and writing, as the child Mozart took to music. When I was about six someone gave me a hand-printing set, and I had my introduction to moveable type. While most normal, healthy extroverts were out robbing birds' nests and setting fire to small buildings, I was setting type, copying the headlines in the newspapers and so on. I was not very gregarious at that age. Instead of team sports, I went in for solitary riding. I had a horse before I had a pony. If there was a note of pious disapproval in my reference to boys who robbed birds' nests, I hasten to disavow it. I didn't steal the eggs from the nests—I shot the birds. Also, my need for companionship was satisfied at home, since I was the first-born of a brood of six sons and two daughters, and whether you pronounce it privvacy or pryvacy, it's a rare treat in a family so large. My father was a surgeon, and presumably knew what caused babies, but it didn't seem to make much difference. In New York, by the way, there is a young and pretty actress who has six children, and when someone said to her that she must be either a Catholic or a sex maniac, she replied that she was both. Like my father.

I, by the way, have one daughter. Her husband is an officer in the Navy and she lives on the Island of Guam. They have been married since last September, mind you, and I am not yet a grandfather. I present this vital statistic to show that not all the young people today are in as much of a hurry as we sometimes believe. Not even the United States Navy.

Did you want me to come here today and inflict upon you a quarter of an hour of esoteric dissertation on the art of writing? As I turn into the home stretch it occurs to me that the general tone of my remarks has been, to say the least, informal and non-intellectual, and that one or two of you may feel that you have not been given your money's worth. If that is the case, I'm sorry. As they say in the courts, I plead guilty with an explanation. As I said a while ago, this is my debut as a public speaker in your country—and very likely to be my farewell appearance as well. I never make speeches at home, or give interviews or appear on the radio or the TV. I am doing it now because my friends at Hodder & Stoughton and the New English Library are very persuasive, and they are convinced—without quite convincing me—that an author's personal appearance does a lot to help sell his books. I was strongly tempted to point out that my books have been selling very well in the United Kingdom without benefit of personal appearances to stimulate the sales. I could still argue the point. But I will admit that I could not think of a better excuse for coming to London, and I am very fond of London. Indeed, my favorite cities in the world are London and Edinburgh, and if I had to live in a city—which thank God I don't—I would settle for, and in, either one. Therefore it is no great hardship to make the journey. However, I know that I am a terrible public speaker, and when I have listened to myself on tape recordings I am appalled by the gruff sound of my voice and my Pennsylvania twang. Even if my father had sent me to Stoneyhurst and Oxford I'd probably still speak the way I do, which is all right at home, where we have had to listen to Wendell L. Willkie and Lyndon B. Johnson, but not all right for an English audience accustomed to the mellifluous Olivier, the clipped Coward, and the plastic accents of the B. B. C. With that handicap in mind I had to try to overcome the disadvantage of *how* I was going to speak by what I had to say.

Well, I could be literary, or literahry. I could offer you a quarter of an hour of literary comments and observations so profound that they could be embalmed in the *Times Literary Supplement*. Or, I could be controversial, by saying disrespectful things about Mr. Toynbee and Sir Charles Snow, among others. Now I have never been one to avoid controversy, literary or otherwise. I have been mentioned in certain dispatches for my recklessness in that regard, and for an essentially peace-loving man I seem to have attracted more than my share of hostility, and expect that I shall continue to do so till my dying day. There are a few scores to settle with the Englishmen who come to the United States (many of them, I regret to say, giving every appearance of taking up permanent residence) and tell us what's wrong with us. You have exported some beauties that you must have been glad to get rid of, if only temporarily. But there is a time and a place for everything, as my grandmother used to say, and as

I am sure your grandmother used to say. Maybe your grandmother said it first. In any event, I decided that this event was not the one at which to hold forth on literary technology or Mr. Toynbee or the situation in Rhodesia or the offensiveness of some of your expatriates. I could touch on all these matters in a way that would give you a strong hint as to what I believe, and yet manage to avoid putting you to sleep or giving you apoplexy. This, after all, is our first meeting, and if it also turns out to be our last, I still want to feel that the decision not to return was mine and completely unofficial. I have had only the slightest acquaintance with Mr. George Raft, and that in Hollywood thirty years ago.

And so my decision was to prepare a lecture, if you can call it that, which would repay you for the courtesy—and the curiosity—of coming to break bread with me. As Mr. Pepys would say, I did on my good suit, I scraped my face, and here I am, shirking my duty as a visiting American author by not pointing out the things that you should change. My American publisher sometimes declares that I have mellowed. Maybe so. If you are mellow, you do not bellow, and I may have done enough bellowing thirty years ago, in my lectures at the 400 Club and the Savoy Grill, to last me a lifetime. Today, not chronologically today but at this stage of my life, I am too full of admiration for the English people to make sensational criticisms for the sake of sensationalism. I am perfectly content to be what I am, a middle-class American, impulsively chauvinistic, and more than satisfied with what happened in 1776. But because I am a middle-class American, and sixty-two years old, I do not feel that I lose face by publicly acknowledging our debt to the English middle class. From you we acquired a sense of decency and fair play, respect for the rule of law, and standards of conduct that add up to civilized behavior. We inherited these virtues and we do not always follow the rules or meet the standards, and neither do you. But they came from you. Britain is the home of the middle class, and in the middle class resides middle thinking and middle behavior, the kind of middle thinking that you return to after too much hope, too much despair, too much action to the right and too much action to the left, too much abandonment of the good and decent things that belonged to the past—for God knows none of us can say what good and decent things belong to the future, or if they do. I am not here to seek to change anything, if change means—as it does—to steer you away from one course into another. That would be the sort of impudence that I deplore in some of your intellectual exports to my country. But I cannot in conscience pass up this opportunity, in this one little minute, to try to restimulate your pride in yourselves and in what your ancestors gave to the world, the strong self-respect that enabled you to respect one another, by habit if not by instinct to respect each other's small rights—as in good manners—and thus to respect each other's larger rights, as demonstrated by observance of the rule of law and the implicit right to change the law, any law.

I am going home the day after tomorrow, to go back to work as a social historian. Thank you.

These remarks were read by John O'Hara on 3 May 1967 at a Foyle's luncheon in London marking publication of the Four Square edition of The Lockwood Concern.

Books

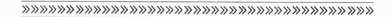

APPOINTMENT
IN SAMARRA

A NOVEL BY JOHN O'HARA

DEATH SPEAKS: There was a merchant in Bagdad who sent his
servant to market to buy provisions and in a little while the servant
came back, white and trembling, and said, Master, just now when I
was in the market-place I was jostled by a woman in the crowd and
when I turned I saw it was Death that jostled me. She looked at me
and made a threatening gesture; now, lend me your horse, and I
will ride away from this city and avoid my fate. I will go to
Samarra and there Death will not find me. The merchant lent him
his horse, and the servant mounted it, and he dug his spurs in its
flanks and as fast as the horse could gallop he went. Then the merchant went down to the market-place and he saw me standing in
the crowd and he came to me and said, Why did you make a threatening gesture to my servant when you saw him this morning? That
was not a threatening gesture, I said, it was only a start of surprise.
I was astonished to see him in Bagdad, for I had an appointment
with him tonight in Samarra. —W. SOMERSET MAUGHAM

HARCOURT, BRACE AND COMPANY
NEW YORK

I. APPOINTMENT IN SAMARRA (1934)

1A [i–viii] [1–2] 3–301 [302–304]
[1–19]^8 [20]^4
On copyright page: 'first edition'
Erratum slip pasted to dedication page.
Published 16 August 1934.
Also advance copies in pictorial wrappers.
5 Harcourt, Brace printings, 1934–1935.

1B New York: Grosset & Dunlap, [1936]. 2 printings?

1C New York: Dover, 1946.

1D New York: Duell, Sloan & Pearce, [1946?].

1E   New York & Cleveland: World, [1947].

1F   New York: Modern Library, [1953]. #42. "With a New Foreword By The Author." 9 printings, 1954–1964.

*1G   New York: Literary Guild, 1963.

*1H   New York: Doubleday Dollar Book Club, 1964.

2   London: Faber & Faber, [1935]. 9 printings, 1935–1965.

3   New York: Pocket Books, [1939]. #27. 2 printings in 1939. Also in paperback, 1961.

*4   Harmondsworth, Middlesex: Penguin, [1944].

5   New York: Penguin, [1945]. #563. 2 printings in 1945.

6   Stockholm & London: Continental Book Co., [1948]. Zephyr #199.

7   New York: Signet, [1954]. #766. 11 printings, 1945–1963.

8   London: Pan, [1958]. #G107.

9   New York: Signet, [1963]. #CP177.

10   London: Corgi, [1965]. #FN7203. 3 printings, 1965–1967.

11   New York: Bantam, [1966]. #S3094. 5 printings.

      Included with *Butterfield 8* and *Hope of Heaven* (1968) . See C6.

THE
DOCTOR'S SON
AND OTHER STORIES
BY JOHN O'HARA

HARCOURT, BRACE AND COMPANY

NEW YORK

II. THE DOCTOR'S SON AND OTHER STORIES (1935)

1 [i–viii] [1–2] 3–294 [295–296]
   [1–19]^8
   On copyright page: 'first edition'
   Published 21 February 1935.
   2 Harcourt, Brace printings in 1935.
   37 stories: "The Doctor's Son," "Early Afternoon," "Pleas-
   ure," "New Day," "The Man Who Had to Talk to
   Somebody," "Mary," "Ella and the Chinee," "Ten
   Eyck or Pershing? Pershing or Ten Eyck?" "Alone,"
   "Coffee Pot," "The Girl Who Had Been Presented,"
   "Mort and Mary," "On His Hands," "It Wouldn't

Break Your Arm," "I Never Seen Anything Like It," "Lombard's Kick," "Frankie," "Mr. Cass and the Ten Thousand Dollars," "Of Thee I Sing, Baby," "Screen Test," "Mr. Sidney Gainsborough: Quality Pictures," "Mr. Cowley and the Young," "Never a Dull Moment," "Master of Ceremonies," "Mrs. Galt and Edwin," "Hotel Kid," "Dr. Wyeth's Son," "Except in My Memory," "The Public Career of Mr. Seymour Harrisburg," "Straight Pool," "Back in New Haven," "Salute a Thoroughbred," "All the Girls He Wanted," "Sportmanship," "In the Morning Sun," "It Must Have Been Spring," "Over the River and Through the Wood."

2   New York: Avon, [1943]. 28 stories.

3   New York: Editions for the Armed Services, [c.1945]. #979. 28 stories.

4   New York: Avon, [   ]. #J511. 28 stories.

See *All the Girls He Wanted* (1949) and *The Great Short Stories of John O'Hara* (1956).

Butterfield 8

A NOVEL BY JOHN O'HARA

Starting on December 16, a distinguishing
numeral will be added to, and become part of,
each central office name in New York City.
For example:

HANover will become HAnover 2

[From an advertisement of the New York
Telephone Company, December 8, 1930.]

HARCOURT, BRACE AND COMPANY

NEW YORK

III. BUTTERFIELD 8 (1935)

1A   [i–iv] [1–2] 3–310 [311–316]
     [1–20]⁸
     On copyright page: *'first edition'*
     Published 17 October 1935.
     2 Harcourt, Brace printings in 1935.

1B   New York: Grosset & Dunlap, [1937].

1C   New York: Modern Library, [1952]. #323. 4 printings,
     1952–1970. Also Modern Library Paperback #P32
     (1957) ; 5 printings, 1957–1960. Vintage paperback
     #V-49; 2 printings, 1966–1969.

2   New York: Editions for the Armed Services, [c.1945]. #799.

3   New York: Avon, [1946]. #94. 9 printings, 1946–1959. Also New York: Shakespeare House, [1951].

4   London: Cresset, 1951. Reprinted in 1969 by Barrie & Rockliff The Cresset Press.

5   Harmondsworth, Middlesex: Penguin, [1960]. #1469. 4 printings, 1960–1964.

6   New York: Bantam, [1960]. #H2104. 18 printings, 1960–1965.

Included in *Here's O'Hara* (1946) . See C1.

Serialized in the *New York Post,* November 1949.

Included with *Appointment in Samarra* and *Hope of Heaven* (1968) . See C6.

HOPE of HEAVEN

BY JOHN O'HARA

Harcourt, Brace and Company   New York

IV. HOPE OF HEAVEN   (1938)

1   [i–iv] [1–2] 3–182 [183–188]
    [1–12]⁸
    On copyright page: 'first edition'
    Published 17 March 1938.
      2 Harcourt, Brace printings in 1938.

2   London: Faber & Faber, [1939]. With 36 stories. Reprinted
      1953.

3   New York: Avon, [1946]. Avon Short Story Monthly #29.
      Omits final chapter. With 4 stories.

4   New York: Avon, [1947]. #144. Omits final chapter. Re-
      printed 1950.

5   Toronto: News Stand Library, [1948]. Omits final chapter.

6   New York: Bantam, [1956]. #1422. 14 printings, 1956–1966.

7   London: Panther, [1960].
    #1086. With 36 stories. 3 printings, 1960–1964.

    Included in *Here's O'Hara* (1946). See C1.
    Included with *Appointment in Samarra* and *Butterfield 8* (1968). See C6.

FILES on PARADE

BY JOHN O'HARA

Harcourt, Brace and Company   New York

V. FILES ON PARADE (1939)

1   [i–vi] vii–viii [ix–x] [1–2] 3–277 [278]
    $[1]^8$ $(1_3 + 1)$ $[2–18]^8$
    NOTE: The Foreword, pp. vii–viii, is inserted in all copies
    of the first printing examined.
    On copyright page: *'first edition'*
    Published 21 September 1939.
      3 Harcourt, Brace printings in 1939.
      35 stories: "Price's Always Open," "Trouble in 1949,"
        "The Cold House," "Days," "Are We Leaving Tomor-
        row?" "Portistan on the Portis," "Lunch Tuesday,"
        "Shave," "Sidesaddle," "No Mistakes," "Brother,"

"Saffercisco," "Ice Cream," "Peggy," "And You Want a Mountain," "Pal Joey," "Ex-Pal," "How I Am Now in Chi," "Bow Wow," "Give and Take," "The Gentleman in the Tan Suit," "Good-by, Herman," "I Could Have Had a Yacht," "Richard Wagner: Public Domain?" "Olive," "It Wouldn't Break Your Arm," "My Girls," "No Sooner Said," "Invite," "All the Girls He Wanted," "By Way of Yonkers," "Most Gorgeous Thing," "A Day Like Today," "The Ideal Man," "Do You Like It Here?"

2   New York: Avon, [1943]. Avon Short Story Monthly #2.

See *All the Girls He Wanted* (1949) and *The Great Short Stories of John O'Hara* (1956).

PAL JOEY

BY JOHN O'HARA

Duell, Sloan and Pearce   New York

VI. PAL JOEY (1940)

1   [1–8] 9–18 [19–20] 21–29 [30–32] 33–46 [47–48] 49–61
[62–64] [65–75] [76–78] 79–93 [94–96] 97–105 [106–
108] 109–118 [119–120] 121–127 [128–130] 131–142
[143–144] 145–156 [157–158] 159–168 [169–170] 171–
181 [182–184] 185–195 [196–200]
[1–12]⁸ [13]⁴
On copyright page: *'first edition'*
Published 23 October 1940.
   2 Duell, Sloan and Pearce printings, 1940. 2nd printing
also noted in Grosset & Dunlap dust jacket.
Also advance copies in printed wrappers.

14 stories: "Pal Joey," "Ex-Pal," "How I Am Now in
Chi," "Bow Wow," "Avast and Belay," "Joey on
Herta," "Joey on the Cake Line," "The Erloff,"
"Even the Greeks," "Joey and the Calcutta Club,"
"Joey and Mavis," "A New Career," "A Bit of a
Shock," "Reminiss?"

2   New York: Editions for the Armed Services, [c.1945].
     #897. 2 printings.

3   New York: Penguin, 1946. #580.

4   New York: Dell, [1951?]. #24.

5   London: Cresset, 1952. Reprinted in 1969 by Barrie &
     Rockliff The Cresset Press.

*6   New York: Bantam, 1957. #1679. 5 printings, 1957–1965.

7   London: Panther, [1960]. 3 printings, 1960–1965.

     See next entry for libretto and lyrics.
     Included in *Here's O'Hara* (1946). See C1.

THE LIBRETTO AND LYRICS

PAL JOEY

✪

By JOHN O'HARA

✪

Lyrics by LORENZ HART

✪

Music by RICHARD RODGERS

✪

RANDOM HOUSE · NEW YORK

VII. PAL JOEY—LIBRETTO AND LYRICS (1952)

[i–viii] [1–2] 3–17 [18] 19–37 [38] 39–53 [54] 55–69 [70–72] 73–
   135 [136]
[1–4]¹⁶ [5]⁸; frontispiece and 2 leaves of illustrations inserted
   between pp. 72–73.
Published 4 August 1952.
  1 Random House printing.

PIPE
NIGHT

BY JOHN O'HARA

WITH A PREFACE BY WOLCOTT GIBBS

DUELL, SLOAN AND PEARCE
NEW YORK

VIII. PIPE NIGHT (1945)

1A   [i–viii] ix–xi [xii] xiii–xiv [1–2] 3–205 [206–210]
     $[1]^8 [2–7]^{16} [8]^8$
     Published 24 March 1945.
     6 Duell, Sloan and Pearce printings in 1945.
     31 stories: "Walter T. Carriman," "Now We Know,"
     "Free," "Can You Carry Me?" "A Purchase of Some
     Golf Clubs," "Too Young," "Joey and the Calcutta
     Club," "Summer's Day," "Radio," "Nothing Miss-
     ing," "The King of the Desert," "Bread Alone," "Re-
     union Over Lightly," "Memo to a Kind Stranger,"
     "The Erloff," "Patriotism," "A Respectable Place,"

"The Magical Numbers," "On Time," "Graven Image," "Adventure on the Set," "Platform," "Civilized," "Revenge," "Fire!" "The Lieutenant," "The Next-to-Last Dance of the Season," "Leave," "The Handler," "Where's the Game," "Mrs. Whitman."

1B   New York & Cleveland: World, [1946].

2   New York: Editions for the Armed Services, [c.1945]. #741.

3   London: Faber & Faber, [1946].

4   *Stories of Venial Sin from Pipe Night.* New York: Avon, [c.1947]. #661. 26 stories.

5   *Stories of Venial Sin from "Pipe Night."* New York: Avon, [1952]. 26 stories.

6   New York: Bantam, [1966]. #H3104. 3 printings.

7A   London: Mayflower-Dell, 1963. Reprinted 1966.

7B   London: New English Library, [1969]. #2380.

HELLBOX

John O'Hara

Random House · New York

IX. HELLBOX (1947)

1   [i–x] [1–3] 4–210 [211–214]; first page of each story un-
    numbered.
    [1–7]^{16}
    On copyright page: 'FIRST PRINTING'
    Published 9 August 1947.
      2 Random House printings in 1947.
      26 stories: "Common Sense Should Tell You," "Pard-
    ner," "Someone to Trust," "Horizon," "Like Old
    Times," "Ellie," "Life Among These Unforgettable
    Characters," "War Aims," "Clara," "Secret Meet-
    ing," "Drawing Room B," "The Decision," "Some-

body Can Help Somebody," "The Pretty Daughters," "Everything Satisfactory," "The Moccasins," "Doctor and Mrs. Parsons," "Wise Guy," "The Three Musketeers," "Other Women's Households," "Transaction," "Miss W.," "Time to Go," "A Phase of Life," "The Chink in the Armor," "Conversation in the Atomic Age."

2   New York: Avon, [1949]. Avon Short Story Monthly #45.

3   New York: Avon, [1950]. #293.

4   London: Faber & Faber, [1952].

5   New York: Bantam, [1961]. #A2230. 3 printings.

*6A   London: Mayflower-Dell, 1963. Reprinted in 1966.

6B   London: New English Library, [1969]. #2379.

A RAGE TO LIVE

RANDOM HOUSE · NEW YORK

X. A RAGE TO LIVE (1949)

1A [i–viii] [1–2] 3–246 [247–248] 249–353 [354–356] 357–455
[456–458] 459–590 [591–592]
[1]^{12} [2–19]^{16}
On copyright page: 'FIRST PRINTING'
Published 16 August 1949.
750 copies were goldstamped *'PRESENTATION EDI-
TION'* on the front cover.
8 Random House printings in 1949; 9th printing in
1964.

1B New York: Grosset & Dunlap, [1950].

2 London: Cresset, 1950. Reprinted in 1951.

3   New York: Bantam, [1951]. #F935. 3 printings in 1951.

4   London: Cresset, 1953.

5   New York: Bantam, [1957]. #F1583. 30 printings, 1957–
    1972.

6   London: Panther, [1960]. #1051. 6 printings, 1960–1966.

Book Find Club selection, October 1949. 2 printings,
1949–1950.
Condensed version: *Omnibook*, XII (January 1950),
1–47.

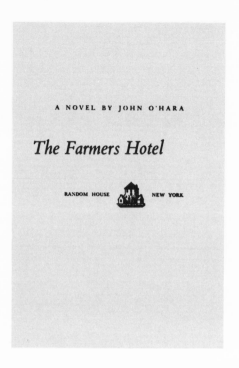

A NOVEL BY JOHN O'HARA

The Farmers Hotel

RANDOM HOUSE · NEW YORK

XI. THE FARMERS HOTEL (1951)

1   [i–vi] [1–2] 3–85 [86–88] 89–134 [135–136] 137–153 [154] [1–5]^{16}
On copyright page: 'FIRST PRINTING'
Published 8 November 1951.
2 Random House printings in 1951.

2   New York: Bantam, [1952]. #1046.

3A   London: Published for The British Publishers Guild by The Cresset Press, [1953].

3B   London: Cresset, 1953. Reprinted in 1969 by Barrie & Rockliff The Cresset Press.

4   New York: Bantam, [1957]. #1594. 18 printings, 1957–
    1970.

5   London: Panther, [1961]. #1186. 3 printings, 1961–1964.

SWEET and SOUR

JOHN O'HARA

RANDOM HOUSE · NEW YORK

XII. SWEET AND SOUR (1954)

1 [i–x] [1–3] 4–162 [163–166]; first page of each piece unnum-
      bered.
   [1–11]⁸
   On copyright page: 'First Printing'
   Published 18 October 1954.
      1 Random House printing.

2 London: Cresset, 1955.

XIII. TEN NORTH FREDERICK (1955)

1A [i–vi] [1–2] 3–389 [390–392] 393–408 [409–410]
    [1–13]^{16}
    On copyright page: 'FIRST PRINTING'
    Published 24 November 1955.
    Also advance copies in wrappers.
    7 Random House printings in 1955–1964.†

1B New York: Grosset & Dunlap, [1957]. '*Sixth Printing.*'

† Note: One or more printings from the Random House plates were
distributed by Sears Readers Club and Sears Selective Readers Service in
1956.

2   London: Cresset, 1956. 2 printings. Reprinted in 1969 by
     Barrie & Rockliff The Cresset Press.

3   New York: Bantam, [1957]. #F1554. 35 printings, 1957–
     1970.

4   London: Panther, [1959]. #959. 12 printings, 1959–1967.

     Published by *Books Abridged* (April 1956).

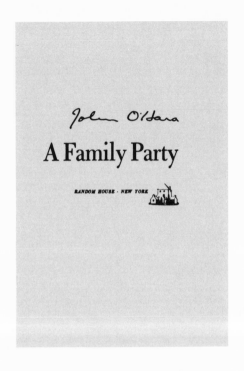

A Family Party

RANDOM HOUSE · NEW YORK

XIV. A FAMILY PARTY (1956)

1   [i–vi] [1–2] 3–64 [65–66]
    [1–3]^{16}
    On copyright page: 'First Printing'
    Published 16 August 1956.
       4 Random House printings in 1956.

2   *Reader's Digest Condensed Books.* Pleasantville, N.Y.:
    Reader's Digest, 1957.

3   London: Cresset, 1957.

4   New York: Bantam, [1957]. #1640. 4 printings.

5   Amsterdam: Meulenhoff, [1962]. 12-page pamphlet of notes
    inserted.

    First published in *Collier's* CXXXVII (2 March 1956),
    34–36, 38, 40–41, 44, 46.

FROM
THE
TERRACE

A NOVEL *by*

John O'Hara

RANDOM HOUSE · NEW YORK

XV. FROM THE TERRACE (1958)

1   [i–vi] [1–2] 3–897 [898]
    [1]⁴ [2–29]¹⁶
    On copyright page: 'FIRST PRINTING'
    Published 27 November 1958.
      2 Random House printings in 1958.

2   London: Cresset, 1959.

3   New York: Bantam, [1960]. #N2026. 34 printings, 1960–
     1972.

4   London: Panther, [1961]. #1251. Reprinted in 1967.

OURSELVES
TO KNOW

A NOVEL *by*
John O'Hara

RANDOM HOUSE · NEW YORK

XVI. OURSELVES TO KNOW (1960)

1A [i–vi] [1–2] 3–408 [409–410]
   [1–13]^{16}
   On copyright page: 'First Printing'
   Published 27 February 1960.
      2 Random House printings in 1960.

1B Offset piracy. Printed in Taiwan, n.d.

2   London: Cresset, 1960.

3   New York: Bantam, [1961]. #S2213. 17 printings, 1961–
      1970.

4   London: Panther, [1962]. #1415. 5 printings, 1962–1965.

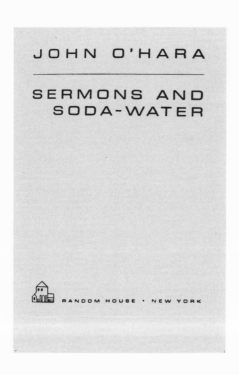

JOHN O'HARA

SERMONS AND
SODA-WATER

RANDOM HOUSE · NEW YORK

XVII. SERMONS AND SODA-WATER (1960)

1A I: *The Girl on the Baggage Truck*
[A–F] [i–viii] ix–xi [xii] [1–2] 3–106 [107–112]
[1]⁸ (1₂ + 1) [2–8]⁸; first and last leaves are paste-down
   endpapers.
On copyright page: 'First Printing'
Unknown number of copies with inserted blank leaf
   signed by the author.
Published 4 November 1960.

II: *Imagine Kissing Pete*
[i–x] [1–2] 3–112 [113–118]
[1–8]⁸; first and last leaves are paste-down endpapers.

On copyright page: 'First Printing'

III: *We're Friends Again*
[i–x] [1–2] 3–110 [111–118]
[1–8]⁸; first and last leaves are paste-down endpapers.
On copyright page: 'First Printing'
3 volumes boxed
   3 Random House printings in 1960.

1B   New York: Random House, [1960?]. 1 volume. 4th printing, but designated 'Third Printing' on copyright page. Dust jacket states 'MARBORO BOOK CLUB EDITION.'

2   London: Cresset, 1961. 3 volumes boxed. 525 numbered and signed copies; certificate of limitation in Volume I.

3   London: Cresset, 1961. 1 volume—trade edition.

4   New York: Bantam, [1962]. #S2338. 9 printings, 1962–1969.

5   London: Corgi, [1963]. #FN7265. 4 printings, 1963–1967.

XVIII. ASSEMBLY (1961)

1A [i–xiv] [1–3] 4–429 [430–434]; first page of each story
    unnumbered.
    [1–14]^{16}
    On copyright page: 'FIRST PRINTING'
    Published 23 November 1961
      3 Random House printings in 1961.
    26 stories: "Mrs. Stratton of Oak Knoll," "The Weakness,"
      "The Man with the Broken Arm," "The Lighter
      When Needed," "The Pioneer Hep-Cat," "The
      Sharks," "The Girl from California," "A Cold
      Calculating Thing," "You Can Always Tell Newark,"

"The High Point," "Call Me, Call Me," "It's Mental Work," "In the Silence," "First Day in Town," "Exactly Eight Thousand Dollars Exactly," "Mary and Norma," "The Cellar Domain," "The Properties of Love," "Reassurance," "The Free," "The Compliment," "Sterling Silver," "The Trip," "In a Grove," "The Old Folks," "A Case History."

1B Offset piracy. Printed in Taiwan, n.d.

1 C *49 Stories.* New York: Modern Library, [1963]. #G-88. *Assembly* and *The Cape Cod Lighter.*

2 London: Cresset, 1962. Also advance copies in printed wrappers.

3 New York: Bantam, [1963]. #S2506. 11 printings, 1963–1969.

4 London: Corgi, [1964]. #FN1484. 4 printings, 1964–1967.

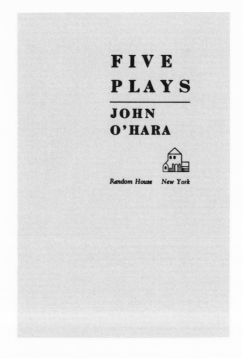

FIVE
PLAYS

JOHN
O'HARA

Random House   New York

XIX. FIVE PLAYS (1961)

1   [A–B] [i–viii] ix–xiv [1–2] 3–85 [86–88] 89–182 [183–184]
        185–302 [303–304] 305–415 [416–418] 419–473 [474–
        480]
     [1–7]¹⁶ [8–9]¹² [10–16]¹⁶
     On copyright page: 'First Printing'
     Published 11 August 1961.
        1 Random House printing.
     "The Farmers Hotel," "The Searching Sun," "The Cham-
     pagne Pool," "Veronique," "The Way It Was."

2   London: Cresset Press, [1961]. Also advance copies in
     printed wrappers.

JOHN O'HARA

THE CAPE COD LIGHTER

RANDOM HOUSE · NEW YORK

XX. THE CAPE COD LIGHTER (1962)

1A [A–B] [i–vi] vii–xiii [xiv–xvi] [1–3] 4–425 [426–430]; first page of each story unnumbered.
[1–14]^{16}
On copyright page: 'FIRST PRINTING'
Published 29 November 1962.
7 Random House printings, 1962–1969.
23 stories: "Appearances," "The Bucket of Blood," "The Butterfly," "Claude Emerson, Reporter," "The Engineer," "The Father," "The First Day," "Jurge Dulrumple," "Justice," "The Lesson," "Money," "The Nothing Machine," "Pat Collins," "The Pro-

fessors," "A Short Walk from the Station," "Sunday
Morning," "The Sun-Dodgers," "Things You Really
Want," "Two Turtledoves," "Winter Dance," "The
Women of Madison Avenue," "You Don't Remember
Me," "Your Fah Neefah Neeface."

1B   *49 Stories.* New York: Modern Library, [1963]. #G-88.

Assembly and *The Cape Cod Lighter.*

2   London: Cresset, [1963]. Reprinted in 1969 by Barrie &
Rockliff The Cresset Press.

3   New York: Bantam, [1964]. #W2718. 3 printings, 1964–
1969.

4   London: Corgi, [1965]. #EN7418. Reprinted in 1967.

THE
BIG LAUGH

A NOVEL *by*

John O'Hara

RANDOM HOUSE · NEW YORK

XXI. THE BIG LAUGH (1962)

1   [i–viii] [1–2] 3–308 [309–312]
    [1–10]^{16}
    On copyright page: 'FIRST PRINTING'
    Published 29 May 1962
      1 Random House printing.

2   London: Cresset Press, [1962].

3   New York: Bantam, [1963]. #S2654. 11 printings, 1963–
    1970.

4   London: Corgi, [1964]. #FN7030.

ELIZABETH
APPLETON

A NOVEL *by*
John O'Hara

RANDOM HOUSE · NEW YORK

XXII. ELIZABETH APPLETON (1963)

1A   [i–viii] [1–2] 3–310 [311–312]
     [1–10]^{16}
     On copyright page: 'FIRST PRINTING'
     Published 4 June 1963.
     5 Random House printings in 1963.

1B   Offset piracy. Printed in Taiwan, n.d.

2   London: Cresset, [1963]. Also advance copies in wrappers.

3   New York: Bantam, [1964]. #N2787. 8 printings, 1964–1969.

4   London: Corgi, [1965]. #XN7251. 3 printings, 1965–1968.

JOHN O'HARA

THE HAT
ON THE BED

RANDOM HOUSE · NEW YORK

XXIII. THE HAT ON THE BED (1963)

1   [i–x] [1–3] 4–405 [406]
[1–13]¹⁶
On copyright page: 'FIRST PRINTING'
Published 28 November 1963.
4 Random House printings, 1963–1964.
24 stories: "Agatha," "Aunt Anna," "Eminent Domain,"
"Exterior: with Figure," "The Flatted Saxophone,"
"The Friends of Miss Julia," "The Glendale People,"
"The Golden," "How Can I Tell You?" "I Know
That, Roy," "John Barton Rosedale, Actors' Actor,"
"The Locomobile," "The Manager," "The Man on

the Tractor," "The Mayor," "Ninety Minutes Away,"
"Our Friend the Sea," "The Public Dorothy," "The
Ride from Mauch Chunk," "Saturday Lunch," "Teddy
and the Special Friends," "The Twinkle in His Eye,"
"The Windowpane Check," "Yucca Knolls."

2   London: Cresset, [1964].

3   New York: Bantam, [1965]. #N2889. 5 printings, 1965–
    1971.

4   London: Corgi, [1966]. #EN7370.

JOHN O'HARA

THE HORSE
KNOWS
THE WAY

Over the river and through the wood
To grandfather's house we'll go;
The horse knows the way
To carry the sleigh,
Through the white and drifted snow.

—Thanksgiving Day.
by LYDIA MARIA CHILD (1802-1880)

RANDOM HOUSE · NEW YORK

XXIV. THE HORSE KNOWS THE WAY (1964)

1A [A–D] [i–v] vi–vii [viii–ix] x [1–3] 4–429 [430–434]; first
page of each story unnumbered.
[1–14]¹⁶
On copyright page: 'FIRST PRINTING'
Limited printing. 250 numbered and signed copies on
laid paper.
Published 26 November 1964.
28 stories: "All Tied Up," "The Answer Depends,"
"Arnold Stone," "At the Window," "Aunt Fran,"
"The Bonfire," "The Brain," "Can I Stay Here?"
"Clayton Bunter," "The Clear Track," "The Gun,"

"The Hardware Man," "His Excellency," "The House on the Corner," "I Can't Thank You Enough," "In the Mist," "I Spend My Days in Longing," "The Jet Set," "The Lawbreaker," "The Madeline Wherry Case," "Mrs. Allanson," "The Pig," "School," "The Staring Game," "The Victim," "What's the Good of Knowing?" "The Whole Cherry Pie," "Zero."

1B   Trade printing. Priority undetermined. Same pagination and collation as limited printing.
On copyright page: 'FIRST PRINTING'
Reprinted once by Random House in 1965.

1C   Offset piracy. Printed in Taiwan, n.d.

2   London: Cresset, [1965].

3   New York: Bantam, [1966]. #N3103. 2 printings.

4   London: Corgi, [1966]. #EN7438. Reprinted once.

the girl's mother ~~kadmumak~~ in all probability had not ~~maxxindmfarminmax~~ been

allowed to marry for love. The ~~dmkingkmd~~ delightful novelty of the use of the

expression, "a real love match," was ~~umoorxicious~~ unintended evidence of the rarity of the

phenomenon; it did not often apply. Sometimes love, always as/promised, ~~dmt~~ came into

being after the marriage was an accomplished fact, and the marriage then could

be considered a happy one; but love itself, ~~wxx~~ could be threatened by the propinquity

that had originally brought it into being.

        Thus Adelaide Lockwood, in love with her husband after the

first months of their marriage, was confused by his unexplained, intense con-

cern for their first two children ~~simile~~ The greatest pleasure in many women's lives was

their right to mother their young, and they mildly resented paternal interference.

The father could stay out of the nursery; time enough to exercise his authority

when the children were grown. Abraham Lockwood, however, had shown an inter-

est and made decisions governing the upbringing of his sons from their birth.

Their diet, their sleeping habits, the temperature of their bath water, the

selection of nurses, the children's exposure to sunlight, the degree and method of pun-

ishment and reward---nothing escaped Abraham Lockwood's attention, and the on-

ly explanation he offered was that he was one of the "new" fathers, who took a

more active part in the raising of the children. Adelaide, unable to protest

on any reasonable grounds, did not accept her husband's explanation, and her

skepticism seemed to be confirmed when their daughter was born and the raising

of the child left entirely to ~~kdmixxidmx~~ the mother. Logically, then, Adelaide

deduced that her husband had ambitions for their sons, but this was as close as

she ever came to comprehending his plan.

        The ~~pkxm~~ evolution of the plan had commenced earlier than

Abraham Lockwood's decision to stay out of Philadelphia society. In spite of

his election to membership in The Ruffes he had ~~mexxer zmgxmdmdmhmmmmhfxxx~~ not long de-

THE
LOCKWOOD
CONCERN

A NOVEL *by*

John O'Hara

RANDOM HOUSE · NEW YORK

XXV. THE LOCKWOOD CONCERN (1965)

1A [i–x] [1–2] 3–269 [270–272] 273–342 [343–344] 345–407
    [408]
    [1]¹⁶ (1₁ + 1) [2–13]¹⁶
    On copyright page: *'First Printing'*
    Limited printing. 300 numbered and signed copies on
    laid paper, boxed.
    Published 25 November 1965.

1B Trade printing. Priority undetermined.
    [i–viii] [1–2] 3–269 [270–272] 273–342 [343–344] 345–407
    [408]
    [1–13]¹⁶

On copyright page: *'First Printing'*
276.10 missing in both limited and trade printings.
3 Random House trade printings, 1965–1966.

1C   London: Hodder & Stoughton, [1965]. 3 printings.

1D   London: The Book Club, [   ].

2   New York: New American Library, [1966]. Signet #Q2876.
4 printings.

3A   London: Four Square, [1966]. Limited distribution.

3B   London: Four Square, [1967]. #1816.

MY TURN

JOHN O'HARA

RANDOM HOUSE · NEW YORK

JOHN O'HARA
WAITING FOR WINTER

 RANDOM HOUSE · NEW YORK

XXVII. WAITING FOR WINTER (1966)

1A [A–F] [i–v] vi [vii–viii] [1–3] 4–466 [467–468]; first page of
each story unnumbered.

[1]¹⁶ (1 + 1₁) [2–15]¹⁶

On copyright page: 'First Printing'

Limited printing. 300 numbered and signed copies on
laid paper, boxed.

Published 24 November 1966.

21 stories: "Afternoon Waltz," "Andrea," "The Assistant,"
"Fatimas and Kisses," "Flight," "The Gambler,"
"The General," "A Good Location," "The Jama,"
"James Francis and the Star," "Late, Late Show,"

"Leonard," "Natica Jackson," "The Neighborhood,"
"The Pomeranian," "The Portly Gentleman," "The
Skeletons," "The Tackle," "The Way to Majorca,"
"The Weakling," "Yostie."

1B Trade printing. Priority undetermined.
[A–D] [i–v] vi [vii–viii] [1–3] 4–466 [467–468]
[1–15]¹⁶
On copyright page: *First Printing*
1 Random House trade printing.

2 London: Hodder & Stoughton, [1967].

3 New York: Bantam, [1967]. #N3537. 8 printings, 1967–
1970.

THE

INSTRUMENT

A NOVEL BY

JOHN O'HARA

RANDOM HOUSE
NEW YORK

XXVIII. THE INSTRUMENT (1967)

1A [i–viii] [1–2] 3–138 [139–140] 141–221 [222–224] 225–297
     [298]
     [1]¹⁶ (1 + 1₁) [2–8]¹⁶ [9]⁸ [10]¹⁶
     On copyright page: *'First Printing'*
     Limited printing. 300 numbered and signed copies on
     laid paper, boxed.
     Published 23 November 1967.

1B Trade printing. Priority undetermined.
     [i–vi] [1–2] 3–138 [139–140] 141–221 [222–224] 225–297
     [298]
     [1–8]¹⁶ [9]⁸ [10]¹⁶

On copyright page: *'First Printing'*
3 Random House trade printings, 1967–1968.

2A   New York: Random House, [1967]. Literary Guild.

2B   New York: Random House, [1968]. Dollar Book Club.

3   London: Hodder & Stoughton, [1968].

4   New York: Bantam, [1969]. #Q4565. 9 printings, 1969–
     1970.

5   London: New English Library, [1969]. #2376.

JOHN O'HARA

AND
OTHER
STORIES

RANDOM HOUSE · NEW YORK

XXIX. AND OTHER STORIES (1968)

1A   [A–D] [i–vii] viii–ix [x–xii] [1–3] 4–336 [337–338]; first
page of each story unnumbered.
[1]¹⁶ (1₁ + 1) [2–11]¹⁶
On copyright page: 'First Printing'
Limited printing. 300 numbered and signed copies on laid
paper, boxed.
Published 28 November 1968.
12 stories: "Barred," "The Broken Giraffe," "The
Farmer," "A Few Trips and Some Poetry," "The
Gangster," "The Gunboat and Madge," "How Old,
How Young," "A Man on a Porch," "Papa Gibraltar,"

"The Private People," "The Strong Man," "We'll Have Fun."

1B Trade printing. Priority undetermined.
[A–B] [i–vii] viii–ix [x–xii] [1–3] 4–336 [337–338] [1–11]¹⁶
On copyright page: *'First Printing'*
2 Random House trade printings, 1968–1969.

1C London: Hodder & Stoughton, [1969].

2 New York: Bantam, [1970]. #Q4816.

3 London: New English Library, [1970]. #2638.

LOVEY CHILDS

A Philadelphian's Story

A NOVEL BY

John O'Hara

RANDOM HOUSE
NEW YORK

XXX. LOVEY CHILDS A PHILADELPHIAN'S STORY (1969)

1A [i–viii] [1–2] 3–249 [250]
    [1]¹⁶ (1 + 1₁) [2–8]¹⁶
    On copyright page: 'FIRST PRINTING'
    Limited printing. 200 numbered and signed copies on laid
        paper, boxed.
    Published 27 November 1969.

1B Trade printing. Priority undetermined. On copyright
        page: 'FIRST PRINTING'
    1 Random House trade printing.
    [i–vi] [1–2] 3–249 [250]
    [1–8]¹⁶

1C   London: Hodder & Stoughton, [1970].

2   New York: Bantam, [1970]. #Q5688. 2 printings.

3   London: New English Library, [1972]. #2801.

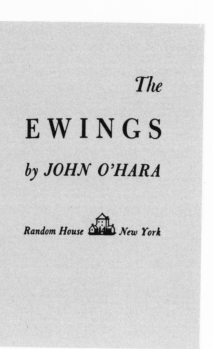

The

EWINGS

by JOHN O'HARA

Random House *New York*

XXXI. THE EWINGS (1972)

1. [i–x] [1–2] 3–310 [311–314]
    Glued, not sewn
    On copyright page: 'First Edition'
    Published 28 February 1972
    2 Random House printings.
    NOTE: The first printing has an error at 231.16–17.

JOHN O'HARA
THE
TIME
ELEMENT

AND OTHER STORIES

RANDOM HOUSE · NEW YORK

XXXII. THE TIME ELEMENT AND OTHER STORIES
(1972)

On copyright page: 'First Edition'
Published 23 November 1972
Foreword by Albert Erskine.
34 stories: "Encounter: 1943," "Conversation at Lunch," "Pil-
grimage," "One for the Road," "The Skipper," "Not
Always," "No Justice," "The Lady Takes an Interest,"
"Interior with Figures," "At the Cothurnos Club," "The
Last of Haley," "Memorial Fund," "The Heart of Lee W.
Lee," "The Brothers," "He Thinks He Owns Me," "The
Dry Murders," "Eileen," "The War," "Nil Nisi," "The
Time Element," "Family Evening," "Requiescat," "The

Frozen Face," "Last Respects," "The Industry and the Professor," "The Busybody," "This Time," "Grief," "The Kids," "The Big Gleaming Coach," "For Help and Pity," "All I've Tried to Be," "The Favor," "That First Husband."

Contributions
to Books and Pamphlets

This section lists only those contributions (fiction and non-fiction) to books and pamphlets that are first appearances in a book or pamphlet. The periodical appearances for these items—when they exist—are noted in the appropriate sections.

1. "Ten Eyck Or Pershing? Pershing Or Ten Eyck" and "The New Office," *The New Yorker Scrapbook*. Garden City, N.Y.: Doubleday, Doran, 1931.

2. "Early Afternoon," *The Best Short Stories of 1932*, ed. Paul Ernest Anderson and Lionel White. New York & London: Putnam's, 1932.

3. "Portrait of a Referee," *These Our Moderns*, ed. Robert E. Galbraith. New York: Nelson, 1933. Also quotes O'Hara on p. 396.

3A. "Are We Leaving Tomorrow?" *Short Stories from The New Yorker*. New York: Simon & Schuster, 1940.

4. "From Winter Quarters, N.Y.," *Ringling Bros And Barnum & Bailey Circus Magazine And Daily Review* (1941).

5. "Is This the Army, Mr. Jones?" *Revue Sketches Vaudeville Comedy Acts . . . Soldier Shows* (Vol. VII, Comedy Sketch Book No. 1). Washington, D.C.: The Infantry Journal, 1943.

6. "The Lieutenant," *Half-A-Hundred Tales By Great American Writers*, ed. Charles Grayson. Philadelphia: Blakiston, [1945]. Included in *Pipe Night*—priority of publication not known.

7. "John O'Hara, Who Talks Like His Stories," *Writers and Writing*, by Robert van Gelder. New York: Scribners, 1946. Interview.

8. "A Visit to 'Quarters,' " *Ringling Bros. & Barnum & Bailey Circus Magazine & Program* (1948).

9. " '21' Is My Club," *The Iron Gate of Jack + Charlie's "21"*. New York: Jack Kriendler Memorial Foundation, 1950.

10. "Foreword," *Monster Rally*, by Chas Addams. New York: Simon & Schuster, [1950]. London: Hamish Hamilton, [1951].

11. Letter to Richard Rodgers, sleeve for *Pal Joey* (Columbia ML 4364).

12. "Joseph Willets Outerbridge," *Harvard Class of 1929 Twenty-fifth Anniversary Report*. Cambridge, Mass.: Printed for the Class, 1954.

13. Interview, *The Writer Observed*, by Harvey Breit. Cleveland & New York: World, [1956].

14. "Remarks on the Novel," *Three Views of the Novel*, by Irving Stone, John O'Hara, and MacKinlay Kantor. Washington: The Library of Congress, 1957.

15. "That First Husband," *The Saturday Evening Post Stories 1959*. Garden City, N.Y.: Doubleday, 1960.

16. Acceptance of the Merit Medal for the Novel, *Proceedings of the American Academy of Arts and Letters and the National Institute of Arts and Letters Second Series Number Fifteen*. New York, 1965.
    See Pennsylvania State University Libraries keepsake.

17. *John O'Hara January 31, 1905 April 11, 1970*. [New York: Random House, 1970]. Keepsake of Random House memorial service; includes letter to Wylie O'Hara Holahan. Printed wrappers—also 45 copies in leather.

18. JOHN O'HARA / 1905–1970 / A Keepsake for a Memorial Exhibit / The Pennsylvania State University Librar-

ies / Tuesday, July 7–Friday, August 14, 1970 / [seal] / In recognition of John O'Hara's services to literature, / and in token of his gifts to The Pennsylvania State / University, we hereby print a facsimile of an address / delivered by Mr. O'Hara on February 29, 1964, on the / occasion of his being awarded the Merit Medal for the / Novel of the American Academy of Arts and Letters.
3-page facsimile of the typescript.

19. "Foreword," *Feet First,* by Ben Finney. New York: Crown, [1971].

20. Review of *Citizen Kane, Film as Film,* ed. Joy Gould Boyum and Adrienne Scott. Boston: Allyn & Bacon, [1971].

Note: The *Ringling Bros. and Barnum & Bailey Circus Magazine* has been treated as a book in items 4 and 8 because it is a program and not a true periodical.

Collections

NOTE: These collections do not include any material by O'Hara published in book form for the first time—with the exception of the Foreword to *Here's O'Hara*.

1. *Here's O'Hara*. New York: Duell, Sloan and Pearce, [1946]. First publication of "Foreword," pp. vii–viii. Includes *Butterfield 8, Hope of Heaven, Pal Joey,* and 20 stories. Reprinted—Cleveland & New York: World, [1946].

2. *All the Girls He Wanted*. New York: Avon, [1949]. Modern Short Story. Monthly #50. 32 stories from *Doctor's Son* and *Files on Parade*. Later edition—New York: Avon, [1951]. #368.

3. *The Great Short Stories of John O'Hara*. New York: Bantam, [1956]. #A1484. 5 printings. 70 stories from *The Doctor's Son* and *Files on Parade*.

4. *Selected Short Stories of John O'Hara*. New York: Modern Library, [1956]. 32 stories, with Introduction by Lionel Trilling.

5. *The O'Hara Generation*. New York: Random House, [1969]. 22 stories, with Introduction by Albert Erskine. Also distributed by the Literary Guild of America and its associated book clubs. Paperback edition—New York: Bantam, [1970]. #Q5546.

6. *Appointment in Samarra Butterfield 8 Hope of Heaven*. New York: Random House, [1968]. 1 volume. Distributed by the Literary Guild of America and its associated book clubs.

Short Stories

》》》

This section lists every short story John O'Hara published, noting the first periodical publication as well as the first collected appearance. Those stories that appeared only in O'Hara's story collections are also included.

1. "The Alumnae Bulletin," *The New Yorker,* IV (5 May 1928), 101.*

2. "Overheard in a Telephone Booth," *The New Yorker,* IV (19 May 1928), 77–78.

3. "Tennis," *The New Yorker,* IV (9 June 1928), 85.

4. "The Follow-up," *The New Yorker,* IV (7 July 1928), 37.

5. "Do You Know ——?" *The New Yorker,* IV (14 July 1928), 41.

6. "Spring 3100," *The New Yorker,* IV (8 September 1928), 56.

7. "A Safe and Sane Fourth," *The New Yorker,* IV (15 September 1928), 79–82. Delphian.†

8. "The Hallowe'en Party," *The New Yorker,* IV (22 September 1928), 84–85. Delphian.

9. "Taking Up Sport," *The New Yorker,* IV (13 October 1928), 58–63. Delphian.

10. "The Coal Fields," *The New Yorker,* IV (20 October 1928), 85–88. Delphian.

* The paginations and occasionally the contents differ in the metropolitan and out-of-town editions of *The New Yorker.*
† One of a Series of stories about the Orange County Afternoon Delphian Society.

11. "The Boss' Present," *The New Yorker*, IV (1 December 1928), 56, 58, 62. Hagedorn & Brownmiller.*

12. "The Yule in Retrospect," *The New Yorker*, IV (29 December 1928), 40–41. Delphian.

13. "Theatre," *The New Yorker*, IV (5 January 1929), 70.

14. "Fifty-cent Meal," *The New Yorker*, IV (12 January 1929), 63–64.

15. "The House Organ," *The New Yorker*, V (23 March 1929), 113–114. Hagedorn & Brownmiller.

16. "Fifteen-Minutes-for-Efficiency," *The New Yorker*, V (30 March 1929), 47–50. Hagedorn & Brownmiller.

17. "A New Apparatus," *The New Yorker*, V (6 April 1929), 61–64. Delphian.

18. "Appreciation," *The New Yorker*, V (13 April 1929), 97–98. Hagedorn & Brownmiller.

19. "Mr. Bonner," *The New Yorker*, V (25 May 1929), 74–75.

20. "Fun for the Kiddies," *The New Yorker*, V (1 June 1929), 76–78. Delphian.

21. "The Tournament," *The New Yorker*, V (8 June 1929), 81–83. Hagedorn & Brownmiller.

22. "Convention," *The New Yorker*, V (15 June 1929), 80–82. Hagedorn & Brownmiller.

23. "Holes in Stockings," *The New Yorker*, V (22 June 1929), 52.

24. "Conditions at the Pool," *The New Yorker*, V (6 July 1929), 45–47. Delphian.

* One of a Series of stories about the Hagedorn & Brownmiller Paint and Varnish Co.

25. "Mr. Rosenthal," *The New Yorker,* V (20 July 1929), 24–25. Hagedorn & Brownmiller.

26. "The Boss Talks," *The New Yorker,* V (3 August 1929), 43–45. Hagedorn & Brownmiller.

27. "Unconditioned Reflexes," *The New Yorker,* V (31 August 1929), 58–61.

28. "Staff Picture," *The New Yorker,* V (7 September 1929), 84–85. Hagedorn & Brownmiller.

29. "Mauve Starts Early Grid Drill," *The New Yorker,* V (21 September 1929), 101–102.

30. "Out of the West," *The New Yorker,* V (28 September 1929), 51–52.

31. "Between the Halves," *The New Yorker,* V (12 October 1929), 85–89.

32. "The Cannons Are a Disgrace," *The New Yorker,* V (19 October 1929), 105–106. Delphian.

33. "Halloween Party," *The New Yorker,* V (26 October 1929), 36. Hagedorn & Brownmiller.

34. "Getting Ready for 1930," *The New Yorker,* V (9 November 1929), 77–78. Hagedorn & Brownmiller.

35. "Americanization," *The New Yorker,* V (23 November 1929), 81–82. Delphian.

36. "Merrie, Merrie, Merrie," *The New Yorker,* V (7 December 1929), 98–100. Delphian.

37. "Memo and Another Memo," *The New Yorker,* V (14 December 1929), 89.

38. "Beaux Arts," *The New Yorker,* V (25 January 1930), 30.

39. "Suits Pressed," *The New Yorker*, V (8 February 1930), 28.

40. "Mr. Cleary Misses a Party," *The New Yorker*, VI (22 February 1930), 90–91. Hagedorn & Brownmiller.

41. "Delphian Hits Girls' Cage-Game Foes," *The New Yorker*, VI (8 March 1930), 84–86.

42. "The Elevator Starter," *The New Yorker*, VI (15 March 1930), 72.

43. "On his Hands," *The New Yorker*, VI (22 March 1930), 54–56. *The Doctor's Son.*

44. "Conversation with a Russian," *The New Yorker*, VI (29 March 1930), 93.

45. "Little Remembrances," *The New Yorker*, VI (12 April 1930), 96–97.

46. "Ten Eyck or Pershing? Pershing or Ten Eyck," *The New Yorker*, VI (19 April 1930), 81–83. *The Doctor's Son.*

47. "A Convert to Equitation," *The New Yorker*, VI (3 May 1930), 97.

48. "Don't Let it Get You," *The New Yorker*, VI (10 May 1930), 51–52.

49. "The New Office," *The New Yorker*, VI (17 May 1930), 98–99. Hagedorn & Brownmiller.

50. "The Girl Who had Been Presented," *The New Yorker*, VI (31 May 1930), 63–64. *The Doctor's Son.*

51. "Most Likely to Succeed," *The New Yorker*, VI (7 June 1930), 38–40.

52. "Paper Drinking Cups?" *The New Yorker*, VI (26 July 1930), 47–49. Hagedorn & Brownmiller.

53. "New Day," *The New Yorker,* VI (23 August 1930), 38–39. *The Doctor's Son.*

54. "The Man Who had to Talk to Somebody," *The New Yorker,* VI (11 October 1930), 77–78. *The Doctor's Son.*

55. "Old Boy," *The New Yorker,* VI (18 October 1930), 28.

56. "Varsity Manager," *The New Yorker,* VI (25 October 1930), 87–88.

57. "Portrait of a Referee," *The New Yorker,* VI (15 November 1930), 80–82.

58. "John," *The New Yorker,* VI (27 December 1930), 28.

59. "Getting a Drink," *The New Yorker,* VI (10 January 1931), 60–61.

60. "One Reason for Betsy's Diffidence," *The New Yorker,* VII (28 February 1931), 65.

61. "Divorce," *The New Yorker,* VII (11 April 1931), 69–71.

62. "The Office Switchboard," *The New Yorker,* VII (25 April 1931), 71–72.

63. "Mary," *The New Yorker,* VII (2 May 1931), 72. *The Doctor's Son.*

64. "Revolt Among the Women," *The New Yorker,* VII (9 May 1931), 73.

65. "Papa and Smoking," *The New Yorker,* VII (16 May 1931), 68–69.

66. "Ninety Cents for a Sardine," *The New Yorker,* VII (23 May 1931), 75.

67. "Help the Younger Element," *The New Yorker,* VII (6 June 1931), 75.

68. "Holiday Plans," *The New Yorker,* VII (27 June 1931), 46–48.

69. "Mort and Mary," *The New Yorker,* VII (19 September 1931), 38–40. *The Doctor's Son.*

70. "Nancy and Mr. Zinzindorf," *The New Yorker,* VII (26 September 1931), 65.

71. "Paolo and Francesca," *The New Yorker,* VII (24 October 1931), 56–57. Delphian.

72. "Let Us Hang on to It," *The New Yorker,* VII (7 November 1931), 56–57. Delphian.

73. ". . . His Partner, Henry T. Collins," *The New Yorker,* VII (28 November 1931), 76–78.

74. "Alone," *Scribner's Magazine,* XC (December 1931), 647–648. *The Doctor's Son.*

75. "Coffee Pot," *The New Yorker,* VII (12 December 1931), 54, 56–57. *The Doctor's Son.*

76. "Ella and the Chinee," *The New Yorker,* VII (23 January 1932), 57–59. *The Doctor's Son.*

77. "Good Evening, Ladies and Gentlemen . . . ," *The New Yorker,* VIII (30 April 1932), 19–20.

78. "Mr. Cass and the Ten Thousand Dollars," *The New Yorker,* VIII (25 June 1932), 53–55. *The Doctor's Son.*

79. "Early Afternoon," *Scribner's Magazine,* XCII (July 1932), 25–26. *The Doctor's Son.*

80. "It Is Easy Enough to Blame Russia," *The New Yorker,* VIII (13 August 1932), 34–36.

81. "I Never Seen Anything Like It," *The New Yorker,* VIII (3 September 1932), 35–36. *The Doctor's Son.*

82. "Lombard's Kick," *The New Yorker,* VIII (24 September 1932), 40–43. *The Doctor's Son.*

83. "Frankie," *The New Yorker*, VIII (8 October 1932), 16–17. *The Doctor's Son*.

84. "Profiles: Of Thee I Sing, Baby," *The New Yorker*, VIII (15 October 1932), 23–25. *The Doctor's Son*.

85. "Screen Test," *The New Yorker*, VIII (3 December 1932), 44–48. *The Doctor's Son*.

86. "Mr. Sidney Gainsborough: Quality Pictures," *The New Yorker*, VIII (17 December 1932), 36–40. *The Doctor's Son*.

87. "You Need a Rest," *The New Yorker*, VIII (14 January 1933), 57–58.

88. "Mrs. Galt and Edwin," *The New Yorker*, IX (18 February 1933), 58–61. *The Doctor's Son*.

89. "Mr. Cowley and the Young," *The New Yorker*, IX (24 June 1933), 31–34. *The Doctor's Son*.

90. "Never a Dull Moment," *The New Yorker*, IX (8 July 1933), 28–30. *The Doctor's Son*.

91. "Hotel Kid," *Vanity Fair*, XLI (September 1933), 4b, 4e. *The Doctor's Son*.

92. "If I Was Brought Up a Holy Roller," *The New Yorker*, IX (16 September 1933), 54–55.

93. "My Friend in Washington," *The New Yorker*, IX (23 September 1933), 20.

94. "The Tenacity of Mr. Crenshaw," *The New Yorker*, IX (30 September 1933), 67–68.

95. "Dynamite Is Like a Mill Pond," *The New Yorker*, IX (14 October 1933), 44–47.

96. "Mrs. McMorrow," *The New Yorker*, IX (18 November 1933), 48–55.

97. "Master of Ceremonies," *The New Yorker*, IX (25 November 1933), 40–43. *The Doctor's Son.*

98. "Straight Pool," *The New Yorker*, IX (16 December 1933), 38–42. *The Doctor's Son.*

99. "Pleasure," *The New Yorker*, X (10 March 1934), 70–73. *The Doctor's Son.*

100. "The Deke Flag." *The New Yorker*, X (24 March 1934), 81–82.

101. "It Must Have Been Spring," *The New Yorker*, X (21 April 1934), 101–104. *The Doctor's Son.*

102. "Sportsmanship," *The New Yorker*, X (12 May 1934), 95–99. *The Doctor's Son.*

103. "In the Morning Sun," *The New Yorker*, X (14 July 1934), 15–17. *The Doctor's Son* and *Files on Parade.*

104. "Dr. Wyeth's Son," *The New Yorker*, X (28 July 1934), 25–26. *The Doctor's Son.*

105. "Salute a Thoroughbred," *The New Yorker*, X (1 September 1934), 17–18. *The Doctor's Son.*

106. "Teddy and Ann," *The New Yorker*, X (15 September 1934), 80–81.

107. "All the Girls he Wanted," *Harper's Bazar*, #2664 (October 1934), 175–176, 179. *The Doctor's Son* and *Files on Parade.*

108. "Back in New Haven," *The New Yorker*, X (6 October 1934), 23–24. *The Doctor's Son.*

109. "Except in My Memory," *Harper's Bazar*, # 2665 (November 1934), 149, 152. *The Doctor's Son.*

110. "Over the River and Through the Wood," *The New Yorker*, X (15 December 1934), 23–25. *The Doctor's Son.*

111. "It Wouldn't Break Your Arm," *Harper's Bazar,* # 2667 (January 1935), 138, 140. *The Doctor's Son* and *Files on Parade.*

112. "You Know How to Live," *The New Yorker,* X (2 February 1935), 20–21.

113. "I Could Have Had a Yacht," *The New Yorker,* XI (6 April 1935), 19. *Files on Parade.*

114. "Ice Cream," *The New Yorker,* XI (20 July 1935), 39–41. *Files on Parade.*

115. "Olive," *The New Yorker,* XI (17 August 1935), 13–15. *Files on Parade.*

116. "The Gentleman in the Tan Suit," *The New Yorker,* XI (7 September 1935), 21–22. *Files on Parade.*

117. "Portistan on the Portis," *The New Yorker,* XI (23 November 1935), 17–18. *Files on Parade.*

118. "Stand-Up," *Collier's,* XCVI (30 November 1935), 17.

119. "The Doctor's Son," *The Doctor's Son.*

120. "The Public Career of Mr. Seymour Harrisburg," *The Doctor's Son.* Unlocated—possibly from *Brooklyn Daily Eagle.*

121. "Most Gorgeous Thing," *The New Yorker,* XII (7 March 1936), 23–24. *Files on Parade.*

122. "Saffercisco," *The New Yorker,* XII (11 April 1936), 14. *Files on Parade.*

123. "Brother," *The New Yorker,* XII (18 July 1936), 23–24. *Files on Parade.*

124. "Pretty Little Mrs. Harper," *Scribner's Magazine,* C (August 1936), 92–93.

125. "Give and Take," *The New Yorker,* XII (13 February 1937), 17–18. *Files on Parade.*

126. "By Way of Yonkers," *The New Yorker,* XIII (27 February 1937), 28–30. *Files on Parade.*

127. "Shave," *The New Yorker,* XIII (20 March 1937), 22–23. *Files on Parade.*

128. "Lunch Tuesday," *The New Yorker,* XIII (3 April 1937), 18–20. *Files on Parade.*

129. "Peggy," *The New Yorker,* XIII (17 April 1937), 24. *Files on Parade.*

130. "My Girls," *The New Yorker,* XIII (29 May 1937), 17–18. *Files on Parade.*

131. "No Sooner Said," *The New Yorker,* XIII (31 July 1937), 13–14. *Files on Parade.*

132. "Price's Always Open," *The New Yorker,* XIII (14 August 1937), 15–17. *Files on Parade.*

133. "Goodbye, Herman," *The New Yorker,* XIII (4 September 1937), 17–18. *Files on Parade.*

134. "Are We Leaving Tomorrow?" *The New Yorker,* XIV (19 March 1938), 17–18. *Files on Parade.*

135. "The Cold House," *The New Yorker,* XIV (2 April 1938), 15–16. *Files on Parade.*

136. "Days," *The New Yorker,* XIV (30 April 1938), 21. *Files on Parade.*

137. "And You Want a Mountain," *The New Yorker,* XIV (11 June 1938), 22–23. *Files on Parade.*

138. "A Day Like Today," *The New Yorker,* XIV (6 August 1938), 14–15. *Files on Parade.*

139. "Richard Wagner: Public Domain?" *The New Yorker,*
XIV (3 September 1938) , 14. *Files on Parade.*

140. "No Mistakes," *The New Yorker,* XIV (17 September
1938) , 18–20. *Files on Parade.*

141. "Pal Joey," *The New Yorker,* XIV (22 October 1938) ,
23–24. *Files on Parade* and *Pal Joey.*

141A. "Trouble in 1949," *Harper's Bazaar,* #2716 (November
1938) , 110–111, 130, 132. *Files on Parade.*

142. "Sidesaddle," *The New Yorker,* XIV (5 November
1938) , 21–22. *Files on Parade.*

143. "Ex-Pal," *The New Yorker,* XIV (26 November 1938) ,
20–21. *Files on Parade* and *Pal Joey.*

144. "Invite," *The New Yorker,* XIV (10 December 1938) ,
27–28. *Files on Parade.*

145. "Do You Like it Here?" *The New Yorker,* XV (18 February 1939) , 17–18. *Files on Parade.*

146. "How I Am Now in Chi," *The New Yorker,* XV (1
April 1939) , 19–21. *Files on Parade* and *Pal Joey.*

147. "The Ideal Man," *The New Yorker,* XV (29 April
1939) , 21–22. *Files on Parade.*

148. "Bow Wow," *The New Yorker,* XV (13 May 1939) ,
21–23. *Files on Parade* and *Pal Joey.*

149. "Can You Carry Me?" *The New Yorker,* XV (3 June
1939) , 17–18. *Pipe Night.*

150. "Reunion Over Lightly," *The New Yorker,* XV (29 July
1939) , 25–26. *Pipe Night.*

151. "Too Young," *The New Yorker,* XV (9 September
1939) , 15–16. *Pipe Night.*

152. "Bread Alone," *The New Yorker*, XV (23 September 1939), 17–18. *Pipe Night.*

153. "Avast and Belay," *The New Yorker*, XV (7 October 1939), 22–23. *Pal Joey.*

154. "Joey on Herta," *The New Yorker*, XV (25 November 1939), 19–22. *Pal Joey.*

155. "Joey on the Cake Line," *The New Yorker*, XV (23 December 1939), 19–20. *Pal Joey.*

156. Entry cancelled.

157. "The Erloff," *The New Yorker*, XV (3 February 1940), 22–23. *Pal Joey* and *Pipe Night.*

158. "Even the Greeks," *The New Yorker*, XVI (2 March 1940), 18–19. *Pal Joey.*

159. "Joey and the Calcutta Club," *The New Yorker*, XVI (30 March 1940), 30–31. *Pal Joey* and *Pipe Night.*

160. "Joey and Mavis," *The New Yorker*, XVI (4 May 1940), 21–22. *Pal Joey.*

161. "A New Career," *The New Yorker*, XVI (13 July 1940), 17–18. *Pal Joey.*

162. "A Respectable Place," *The New Yorker*, XVI (19 October 1940), 26–27. *Pipe Night.*

163. "The King of the Desert," *The New Yorker*, XVI (30 November 1940), 16–17. *Pipe Night.*

164. "A Bit of a Shock," *Pal Joey* (1940).

165. "Reminiss?" *Pal Joey* (1940).

166. "The Magical Numbers," *The New Yorker*, XVI (18 January 1941), 18–19. *Pipe Night.*

167. "Nothing Missing," *The New Yorker*, XVII (14 June 1941), 21–23. *Pipe Night.*

168. "Adventure on the Set," *The New Yorker*, XVII (15 November 1941), 26–27. *Pipe Night*.

169. "Summer's Day," *The New Yorker*, XVIII (29 August 1942), 15–16. *Pipe Night*.

170. "Graven Image," *The New Yorker*, XIX (13 March 1943), 17–18. *Pipe Night*.

171. "Radio," *The New Yorker*, XIX (22 May 1943), 20–21. *Pipe Night*.

172. "Now We Know," *The New Yorker*, XIX (5 June 1943), 19–20. *Pipe Night*.

173. "The Next-to-Last Dance of the Season," *The New Yorker*, XIX (18 September 1943), 22–24. *Pipe Night*.

174. "Revenge," *Collier's*, CXII (25 September 1943), 21. *Pipe Night*.

175. "Walter T. Carriman," *The New Yorker*, XIX (16 October 1943), 23–27. *Pipe Night*.

176. "Memo to a Kind Stranger," *Collier's*, CXII (6 November 1943), 19. *Pipe Night*.

177. "The Lieutenant," *The New Yorker*, XIX (13 November 1943), 22–23. *Pipe Night*.

178. "Civilized," *The New Yorker*, XIX (4 December 1943), 32–33. *Pipe Night*.

179. "On Time," *Collier's*, CXIII (8 April 1944), 72. *Pipe Night*.

180. "Conversation at Lunch," *Good Housekeeping*, CXIX (July 1944), 28. *The Time Element*.

181. "Name in the Book," *Good Housekeeping*, CXIX (December 1944), 38, 172–173.

182. "Leave," *Collier's*, CXIV (2 December 1944), 13. *Pipe Night.*

183. "Mrs. Whitman," *The New Yorker*, XX (27 January 1945), 20–22. *Pipe Night.*

184. "The Pretty Daughters," *The New Yorker*, XXI (3 March 1945), 24–26. *Hellbox.*

185. "War Aims," *The New Yorker*, XXI (17 March 1945), 27–28. *Hellbox.*

186. "Wise Guy," *The New Yorker*, XXI (26 May 1945), 20–21. *Hellbox.*

187. "Horizon," *The New Yorker*, XXI (23 June 1945), 18. *Hellbox.*

188. "Life Among these Unforgettable Characters," *The New Yorker*, XXI (25 August 1945), 19–20. *Hellbox.*

189. "Fire!" *Pipe Night* (1945).

190. "Free," *Pipe Night* (1945).

191. "The Handler," *Pipe Night* (1945).

192. "Patriotism," *Pipe Night* (1945).

193. "Platform," *Pipe Night* (1945).

194. "A Purchase of Some Golf Clubs," *Pipe Night* (1945).

195. "Where's the Game," *Pipe Night* (1945).

196. "Conversation in the Atomic Age," *The New Yorker*, XXI (12 January 1946), 22–23. *Hellbox.*

197. "Common Sense Should Tell You," *The New Yorker*, XXI (9 February 1946), 20–22. *Hellbox.*

198. "Doctor and Mrs. Parsons," *The New Yorker*, XXII (23 February 1946), 29–31. *Hellbox.*

199. "Everything Satisfactory," *The New Yorker*, XXII (23 March 1946), 25–26. *Hellbox.*

200. "Like Old Times," *The New Yorker*, XXII (13 April 1946), 29–30. *Hellbox.*

201. Entry cancelled.

202. "Clara," *The New Yorker*, XXII (27 April 1946), 21–23. *Hellbox.*

203. "The Decision," *The New Yorker*, XXII (18 May 1946), 23–25. *Hellbox.*

204. "Secret Meeting," *The New Yorker*, XXII (6 July 1946), 18–19. *Hellbox.*

205. "The Three Musketeers," *The New Yorker*, XXII (28 September 1946), 25–26. *Hellbox.*

206. "Ellie," *The New Yorker*, XXII (19 October 1946), 29–30. *Hellbox.*

207. "Pilgrimage," *The New Yorker*, XXII (9 November 1946), 29–32. *The Time Element.*

208. "One for the Road," *The New Yorker*, XXII (30 November 1946), 37–38.

209. "Not Always," *The New Yorker*, XXII (11 January 1947), 23–24. *The Time Element.*

210. "The Moccasins," *The New Yorker*, XXII (25 January 1947), 20–22. *Hellbox.*

211. "Pardner," *The New Yorker*, XXIII (22 February 1947), 24–26. *Hellbox.*

212. "Someone to Trust," *The New Yorker*, XXIII (22 March 1947), 31–33. *Hellbox.*

213. "Drawing Room B," *The New Yorker*, XXIII (19 April 1947), 25–28. *Hellbox.*

214. "Miss W.," *The New Yorker*, XXIII (3 May 1947), 29–30. *Hellbox*.

215. "Other Women's Households," *The New Yorker*, XXIII (24 May 1947), 32–34. *Hellbox*.

216. "The Lady Takes an Interest," *The New Yorker*, XXIII (28 June 1947), 22–23. *The Time Element*.

217. "Interior with Figures," *The New Yorker*, XXIII (19 July 1947), 22–24. *The Time Element*.

218. "The Last of Haley," *The New Yorker*, XXIII (30 August 1947), 21–23. *The Time Element*.

219. "The Heart of Lee W. Lee," *The New Yorker*, XXIII (13 September 1947), 29–31. *The Time Element*.

220. "The Dry Murders," *The New Yorker*, XXIII (18 October 1947), 33–34. *The Time Element*.

221. "Eileen," *The New Yorker*, XXIII (20 December 1947), 25–26. *The Time Element*.

222. "The Chink in the Armor," *Hellbox* (1947).

223. "A Phase of Life," *Hellbox* (1947).

224. "Somebody Can Help Somebody," *Hellbox* (1947).

225. "Time to Go," *Hellbox* (1947).

226. "Transaction," *Hellbox* (1947).

227. "Nil Nisi," *The New Yorker*, XXIII (10 January 1948), 23–25. *The Time Element*.

228. "Requiescat," *The New Yorker*, XXIV (3 April 1948), 27–30. *The Time Element*.

229. "The Frozen Face," *The New Yorker*, XXV (23 April 1949), 22–24. *The Time Element*.

230. "The Industry and the Professor," *The New Yorker,* XXV (16 July 1949), 16–20. *The Time Element.*

231. "Grief," *The New Yorker,* XXV (22 October 1949), 28–29. *The Time Element.*

232. "The Kids," *The New Yorker,* XXV (26 November 1949). 32–34. *The Time Element.*

233. "The Favor," *The Princeton Tiger,* LXIII (March–April 1952), 8–10. *The Time Element.*

234. "A Family Party," *Collier's,* CXXXVII (2 March 1956), 34–36, 38, 40–41, 44, 46.

235. "That First Husband," *Saturday Evening Post,* CCXXXII (21 November 1959), 23–24, 52. *The Time Element.*

236. "Imagine Kissing Pete," *The New Yorker,* XXXVI (17 September 1960), 43–134. *Sermons and Soda-Water.*

237. "It's Mental Work," *The New Yorker,* XXXVI (26 November 1960), 50–56. *Assembly.*

238. "Exactly Eight Thousand Dollars Exactly," *The New Yorker,* XXXVI (31 December 1960), 24–26. *Assembly.*

239. "The Girl on the Baggage Truck," *Sermons and Soda-Water.*

240. "We're Friends Again," *Sermons and Soda-Water.*

241. "The Cellar Domain," *The New Yorker,* XXXVI (11 February 1961), 28–34. *Assembly.*

242. "Sterling Silver," *The New Yorker,* XXXVII (11 March 1961), 38–42. *Assembly.*

243. "The Man with the Broken Arm," *The New Yorker,* XXXVII (22 April 1961), 42–47. *Assembly.*

244. "The Girl from California," *The New Yorker*, XXXVII (27 May 1961), 34–42. *Assembly*.

245. "The Weakness," *The New Yorker*, XXXVII (8 July 1961), 23–29. *Assembly*.

246. "Mary and Norma," *The New Yorker*, XXXVII (5 August 1961), 22–26. *Assembly*.

247. "The Trip," *The New Yorker*, XXXVII (23 September 1961), 39–42. *Assembly*.

248. "Call Me, Call Me," *The New Yorker*, XXXVII (7 October 1961), 56–58. *Assembly*.

249. "The Father," *The New Yorker*, XXXVII (28 October 1961), 48–49. *The Cape Cod Lighter*.

250. "Two Turtledoves," *The New Yorker*, XXXVII (23 December 1961), 22–23. *The Cape Cod Lighter*.

251. "A Case History," *Assembly*.

252. "A Cold Calculating Thing," *Assembly*.

253. "The Compliment," *Assembly*.

254. "First Day in Town," *Assembly*.

255. "The Free," *Assembly*.

256. "The High Point," *Assembly*.

257. "In a Grove," *Assembly*.

258. "In the Silence," *Assembly*.

259. "The Lighter When Needed," *Assembly*.

260. "Mrs. Stratton of Oak Knoll," *Assembly*.

261. "The Old Folks," *Assembly*.

262. "The Pioneer Hep-Cat," *Assembly*.

263. "The Properties of Love," *Assembly.*

264. "Reassurance," *Assembly.*

265. "The Sharks," *Assembly.*

266. "You Can Always Tell Newark," *Assembly.*

267. "Sunday Morning," *The New Yorker,* XXXVII (13 January 1962), 24–26. *The Cape Cod Lighter.*

268. "The Women of Madison Avenue," *The New Yorker,* XXXVII (10 February 1962), 32–33. *The Cape Cod Lighter.*

269. "A Short Walk from the Station," *The New Yorker,* XXXVIII (24 February 1962), 32–34. *The Cape Cod Lighter.*

270. "Money," *The New Yorker,* XXXVIII (24 March 1962), 38–46. *The Cape Cod Lighter.*

271. "The Bucket of Blood," *The New Yorker,* XXXVIII (25 August 1962), 31–62. *The Cape Cod Lighter.*

272. "Winter Dance," *The New Yorker,* XXXVIII (22 September 1962), 34–36. *The Cape Cod Lighter.*

273. "How Can I Tell You?" *The New Yorker,* XXXVIII (1 December 1962), 57–59. *The Hat on the Bed.*

274. "The Public Dorothy," *The New Yorker,* XXXVIII (15 December 1962), 36–37. *The Hat on the Bed.*

275. "Appearances," *The Cape Cod Lighter.*

276. "The Butterfly," *The Cape Cod Lighter.*

277. "Claude Emerson, Reporter," *The Cape Cod Lighter.*

278. "Jurge Dulrumple," *The Cape Cod Lighter.*

279. "The Engineer," *The Cape Cod Lighter.*

280. "The First Day," *The Cape Cod Lighter.*

281. "Justice," *The Cape Cod Lighter.*

282. "The Lesson," *The Cape Cod Lighter.*

283. "The Nothing Machine," *The Cape Cod Lighter.*

284. "Pat Collins," *The Cape Cod Lighter.*

285. "The Professors," *The Cape Cod Lighter.*

286. "The Sun-Dodgers," *The Cape Cod Lighter.*

287. "Things You Really Want," *The Cape Cod Lighter.*

288. "You Don't Remember Me," *The Cape Cod Lighter.*

289. "Your Fah Neefah Neeface," *The Cape Cod Lighter.*

290. "Saturday Lunch," *The New Yorker*, XXXVIII (12 January 1963), 27–30. *The Hat on the Bed.*

291. "Agatha," *The New Yorker*, XXXIX (23 February 1963), 33–39. *The Hat on the Bed.*

292. "The Glendale People," *The Saturday Evening Post*, CCXXXVI (2 March 1963), 34–41. *The Hat on the Bed.*

293. "John Barton Rosedale, Actors' Actor," *The New Yorker*, XXXIX (16 March 1963), 46–53. *The Hat on the Bed.*

294. "Aunt Anna," *The Saturday Evening Post*, CCXXXVI (23 March 1963), 50–56. *The Hat on the Bed.*

295. "Yucca Knolls," *Show Magazine*, III (April 1963), 85–100. *The Hat on the Bed.*

296. "The Ride from Mauch Chunk," *The Saturday Evening Post*, CCXXXVI (13 April 1963), 38–41. *The Hat on the Bed.*

297. "The Manager," *The New Yorker,* XXXIX (4 May 1963), 42–48. *The Hat on the Bed.*

298. "Exterior: With Figure," *The Saturday Evening Post,* CCXXXVI (1 June 1963), 54–61. *The Hat on the Bed.*

299. "The Flatted Saxophone," *The New Yorker,* XXXIX (1 June 1963), 28–29. *The Hat on the Bed.*

300. "The Man on the Tractor," *The New Yorker,* XXXIX (22 June 1963), 25–30. *The Hat on the Bed.*

301. "The Locomobile," *The New Yorker,* XXXIX (20 July 1963), 22–27. *The Hat on the Bed.*

302. "Our Friend the Sea," *The Saturday Evening Post,* CCXXXVI (24–31 August 1963), 60–65. *The Hat on the Bed.*

303. "The Lawbreaker," *The Saturday Evening Post,* CCXXXVI (16 November 1963), 52–54, 58, 62, 64, 68, 69, 70, 72–77. *The Horse Knows the Way.*

304. "Zero," *The New Yorker,* XXXIX (28 December 1963), 28–32. *The Horse Knows the Way.*

305. "Eminent Domain," *The Hat on the Bed.*

306. "The Friends of Miss Julia," *The Hat on the Bed.*

307. "The Golden," *The Hat on the Bed.*

308. "I Know That, Roy," *The Hat on the Bed.*

309. "The Mayor," *The Hat on the Bed.*

310. "Ninety Minutes Away," *The Hat on the Bed.*

311. "Teddy and the Special Friends," *The Hat on the Bed.*

312. "The Twinkle in His Eye," *The Hat on the Bed.*

313. "The Windowpane Check," *The Hat on the Bed.*

314. "The Whole Cherry Pie," *The Saturday Evening Post,* CCXXXVII (8 February 1964), 32–33. *The Horse Knows the Way.*

315. "At the Window," *The New Yorker,* XL (22 February 1964), 28–32. *The Horse Knows the Way.*

316. "The Hardware Man," *The Saturday Evening Post,* CCXXXVII (29 February 1964), 46–53. *The Horse Knows the Way.*

317. "The Victim," *The Saturday Evening Post,* CCXXXVII (14 March 1964), 46–51. *The Horse Knows the Way.*

318. "Arnold Stone," *The Saturday Evening Post,* CCXXXVII (28 March 1964), 52–59. *The Horse Knows the Way.*

319. "The Answer Depends," *The Saturday Evening Post,* CCXXXVII (18 April 1964), 46–51. *The Horse Knows the Way.*

320. "Can I Stay Here?" *The Saturday Evening Post,* CCXXXVII (16 May 1964), 44–45, 48. *The Horse Knows the Way.*

321. "I Spend My Days in Longing," *The New Yorker,* XL (23 May 1964), 40–46. *The Horse Knows the Way.*

322. "His Excellency," *The Saturday Evening Post,* CCXXXVII (11 July 1964), 56–60. *The Horse Knows the Way.*

323. "The House on the Corner," *The Saturday Evening Post,* CCXXXVII (22 August 1964), 64–66. *The Horse Knows the Way.*

324. "Aunt Fran," *The Saturday Evening Post,* CCXXXVII (15 September 1964), 56–57. *The Horse Knows the Way.*

341. "The Gun," *The Horse Knows the Way.*

342. "I Can't Thank You Enough," *The Horse Knows the Way.*

343. "In the Mist," *The Horse Knows the Way.*

344. "The Jet Set," *The Horse Knows the Way.*

345. "A Good Location," *The New Yorker*, XLI (4 September 1965), 29–31. *Waiting for Winter.*

346. "Leonard," *The New Yorker*, XLII (26 February 1966), 33–37. *Waiting for Winter.*

347. "Afternoon Waltz," *The Saturday Evening Post*, CCXXXIX (23 April 1966), 56–74. *Waiting for Winter.*

348. "Fatimas and Kisses," *The New Yorker*, XLII (21 May 1966), 44–53. *Waiting for Winter.*

349. "Yostie," *The Saturday Evening Post*, CCXXXIX (4 June 1966), 46–62. *Waiting for Winter.*

350. "The Jama," *The Saturday Evening Post*, CCXXXIX (22 October 1966). *Waiting for Winter.*

351. "The Private People," *The Saturday Evening Post*, CCXXXIX (17 December 1966), 56–72. *And Other Stories.*

352. "Andrea," *Waiting for Winter.*

353. "Flight," *Waiting for Winter.*

354. "The General," *Waiting for Winter.*

355. "James Francis and the Star," *Waiting for Winter.*

356. "Late, Late Show," *Waiting for Winter.*

357. "Natica Jackson," *Waiting for Winter.*

358. "The Pomeranian," *Waiting for Winter.*

359. "The Portly Gentleman," *Waiting for Winter.*

360. "The Skeletons," *Waiting for Winter.*

361. "The Way to Majorca," *Waiting for Winter.*

362. "The Weakling," *Waiting for Winter.*

363. "The Gunboat and Madge," *The Saturday Evening Post,* CCXL (25 February 1967), 64–77. *And Other Stories.*

364. "How Old, How Young," *The New Yorker,* XLIII (1 July 1967), 28–32. *And Other Stories.*

365. "Barred," *The Saturday Evening Post,* CCXL (7 October 1967), 60–62. *And Other Stories.*

366. "The Gangster," *The Saturday Evening Post,* CCXL (18 November 1967), 56–66. *And Other Stories.*

367. "Good Samaritan," *The Saturday Evening Post,* CCXLI (30 November 1968), 62–64, 66, 68–70.

368. "The Broken Giraffe," *And Other Stories.*

369. "The Farmer," *And Other Stories.*

370. "A Few Trips and Some Poetry," *And Other Stories.*

371. "A Man on a Porch," *And Other Stories.*

372. "Papa Gibraltar," *And Other Stories.*

373. "The Strong Man," *And Other Stories.*

374. "We'll Have Fun," *And Other Stories.*

375. "At the Cothurnos Club," *Esquire,* LXXVIII (July 1972), 114–115. *The Time Element.* This story and "All I've Tried to Be" appear under *Esquire*'s general title, "The Little Mysteries of Pomp and Circumstance."

376. "All I've Tried to Be," *Esquire,* LXXVIII (July 1972), 115–116, 162–164. *The Time Element.* See #375.

377. "Encounter: 1943," *The Time Element.*

378. "The Skipper," *The Time Element.*

379. "No Justice," *The Time Element.*

380. "Memorial Fund," *The Time Element.*

381. "The Brothers," *The Time Element.*

382. "He Thinks He Owns Me," *The Time Element.*

383. "The War," *The Time Element.*

384. "The Time Element," *The Time Element.*

385. "Family Evening," *The Time Element.*

386. "Last Respects," *The Time Element.*

387. "The Busybody," *The Time Element.*

388. "This Time," *The Time Element.*

389. "The Big Gleaming Coach," *The Time Element.*

390. "For Help and Pity," *The Time Element.*

Articles

1. "A Cub Tells His Story," *Pottsville Journal* (2 May 1925), 17.

2. "Saxophonic Fever," *New York Herald-Tribune* (17 February 1929), II, 7.

3. "The Pennsylvania Irish," *New York Herald-Tribune* (9 March 1930), II, 7.

4. "Dancing School," *New York Herald-Tribune* (3 August 1930), II, 7.

5. "The Decline of Jazz," *New York Herald-Tribune* (14 September 1930), II, 7.

6. "Giants of a Vanished Race," *New York Herald-Tribune* (28 September 1930), II, 7.

7. "Jazz Artists," *New York Herald-Tribune* (14 December 1930), II, 9.

8. "A Jazz Leader," *New York Herald-Tribune* (25 January 1931), II, 9.

9. "Jazz from the West," *New York Herald-Tribune* (1 March 1931), II, 9.

10. "Sing Us the Old Songs," *New York Herald-Tribune* (9 August 1931), II, 9.

11. "When Dinner Coats Were Tucks and Young Men Toddled," *New York Herald-Tribune* (30 August 1931), II, 9.

12. "Football: Up Boston Way," *The New Yorker,* IX (18 November 1933), 30–32.

13. "Football: Four Downs and a Fumble," *The New Yorker,* IX (25 November 1933), 61–62.

14. "Football: Requests and Demands," *The New Yorker,* IX (2 December 1933), 52, 54.

15. "Football: Princeton Visits the Bowl," *The New Yorker,* IX (9 December 1933), 85–87.

16. "Football: The Coming Boom in Stadiums," *The New Yorker,* X (29 September 1934), 30, 32.

17. "Cesar Romero and the Three Dollar Bills," *New York Journal* and *Chicago American* (13 June 1936), Saturday Home Magazine section.

18. "Take It!" *New Republic,* CI (27 December 1939), 287.

19. "In Memory of Scott Fitzgerald: II—Certain Aspects," *New Republic,* CIV (3 March 1941), 311.

20. "Some Fond Recollections of Larry Hart," *New York Times* (27 February 1944), II, 1.

21. "Nothing from Joe?" *Liberty* XXI (9 December 1944), 20, 21.

22. "The Stutz Bearcat," *Holiday,* IV (August 1948), 84, 86–89.

23. "Why Manchester Roots for Its Small-Town Doctor," *New York Daily Mirror* (9 March 1950), 2, 26.

24. "The New Expense-Account Society," *Flair,* I (May 1950), 22–23, 110–111.

25. "Famous Author Writes of His Early Days on Journal; Is Now Big Literary Figure," *Pottsville Journal* (2 October 1950), 5.

26. " 'Joey' Comes of Age," *New York Herald-Tribune* (23 November 1952), IV, 1, 3.

27. "There is Nothing Like a Norfolk," *Holiday,* XIV (September 1953), 14, 17.

28. "Novelist Likes the Film Translation," *New York Herald-Tribune* (18 May 1958), IV, 3.

29. "Don't Say It Never Happened," *New York Herald-Tribune Books* (8 April 1962), 3.

29A. "Bleeck's: John O'Hara Recalls a Cave of Journalism Greats," *New York Herald-Tribune* (24 April 1963), 28.

30. "A Business, And Such a Business," *Baltimore Sun TV Week* (29 November 1964).

31. "The Wayward Reader," *Holiday,* XXXVI (December 1964), 31-34.

32. "Memoirs of a Sentimental Duffer," *Holiday,* XXXVII (May 1965), 66-67, 118, 120, 122.

33. "On Cars and Snobbism," *Holiday,* XL (August 1966), 52-53.

34. "Celibacy, Sacred and Profane," *Holiday,* XLII (August 1967), 28-29.

35. "Hello Hollywood Good-bye," *Holiday,* XLIII (May 1968), 54-55, 125-126, 128-129.

Interviews
and Public Statements

»»»

JOHN O'HARA *says—*

This—APPOINTMENT IN SAMARRA—*is my first novel, and I am finding out things about post-publication events in the life of a novel and of a novelist. The thing people ask most frequently is: "How many copies have you sold?" The next question: "Where did you write the book, and how long did it take?" Well, I began writing it just before Christmas, 1933, and turned in the completed mss. on April 8, 1934. The whole novel was written at night, in a "club hotel" in East 51st Street, between the Third Avenue and Second Avenue Elevated Lines. This proves something. Another thing is that there was only one typescript of* APPOINTMENT IN SAMARRA.

John O'Hara

1. "John O'Hara says—," Unlocated ad for *Appointment in Samarra* (1934).

2. Robert Van Gelder, "John O'Hara, Who Talks Like His Stories," *New York Herald-Tribune Books* (26 May 1940), 12. See B7.

3. Thomas O'Hara, "John O'Hara Interviewed By Brother at Show Here," *Philadelphia Evening Public Ledger* (11 December 1940).

4. Lucius Beebe, "Stage Asides," *New York Herald-Tribune* (12 January 1941), VI, 1–2. Interview about *Pal Joey*.

5. "The Novels Novelists Read, or 'Taking in The Washing,'" *New York Times Book Review* (21 August 1949), 3.

6. Harvey Breit, "Talk With John O'Hara," *New York Times Book Review* (4 September 1949), 11.

7. Benjamin Welles, "John O'Hara And His Pal Joey," *New York Times* (26 January 1951), IX, 2.

8. "Some Authors of 1951 Speaking for Themselves: John O'Hara," *New York Herald-Tribune Book Review* (7 October 1951), 6.

9. William M. Dwyer, "O'Hara Writes Play, Amateurs Stage It," *New York Herald-Tribune* (18 May 1952), IV, 2.

10. Lewis Nichols, "Talk With John O'Hara," *New York Times Book Review* (27 November 1955), 16.

11. John K. Hutchens, "John O'Hara from Pottsville, Pa.," *New York Herald-Tribune Books* (4 December 1955), 2.

12. John K. Hutchens, "Authors, Critics, Speeches, Prizes," *New York Herald-Tribune Book Review* (12 February 1956), 2, 4.

13. Anon. "As 'From the Terrace' Goes to Press: Appointment With O'Hara," *Publishers' Weekly*, CLXXIV (3 November 1958), 22–23.

14. Rollene Waterman, "Appt. with O'Hara," *Saturday Review*, XLI (29 November 1958), 15.

15. "Talk With the Author," *Newsweek*, LII (1 December 1958), 93–94.

16. Maurice Dolbier, "What NBA Means to Some Past Winners," *New York Herald-Tribune Book Review* (1 March 1959), 2, 11.

16A. Anon., "A Writer's Look at his Town, Career and Future," *Princeton Packet* (23 November 1961), 1, 4.

17. Miles A. Smith, "O'Hara Looks at Himself," AP dispatch, January 1962.

18. Lewis Nichols, "In And Out of Books," *New York Times Book Review* (29 July 1962), 8.

19. Anon. "John O'Hara at 58: A Rage to Write," *Newsweek*, LXI (3 June 1963), 53–57.

20. Sam Zolotow, "John O'Hara Finds Playwriting Fun," *New York Times* (29 July 1963), 16.

21. Ray Erwin, "John O'Hara Comes 'Home' to Newspapers," *Editor & Publisher*, XCVII (26 September 1964), 120.

22. Lewis Nichols, "In And Out of Books." *New York Times Book Review* (29 November 1964), 8.

23. Arthur Pottersman, "The world, I think, is better off that I'm a writer," *London Sun* (21 September 1965), 3.

24. Homer Bigart, "Staff of Tribune Sad, Not Shocked," *New York Times* (16 August 1966), 26. Statement on the death of *The New York Herald-Tribune*.

25. Alden Whitman, "O'Hara, in Rare Interview, Calls Literary Landscape Fairly Bleak," *New York Times* (13 November 1967), 45.

26. Alden Whitman, Untitled interview, *New York Times Book Review* (26 November 1967), 5.

27. Don A. Schanche, "John O'Hara Is Alive and Well in the First Half of the Twentieth Century," *Esquire*, CXXII (August 1969), 84–86, 142, 144–149.

Addenda

Jack Keating, "John O'Hara's World of Yale, Society, and Sex," *Cosmopolitan*, CXLIX (September 1960), 59–63.

Kate Lloyd, "On the American Scene: John O'Hara," *Glamour*, XLVII (May 1962), 125, 197.

Published Letters

»»

1. Letter to the Editor, *Time,* IX (9 May 1927), 6.

2. Letter to the Editor, *Time,* XI (23 January 1928), 1.

3. Richard Watts, Jr., "A Defense of the Film Star Who has to Live his Parts," *New York Herald-Tribune* (13 July 1930), VIII, 3. Includes O'Hara letter.

4. Stanley Woodward's column, *New York Herald-Tribune* (16 January 1938), III, 3. Includes O'Hara letter.

5. Letter to the Editor, *New York Herald-Tribune* (3 March 1938), 16.

6. Letter to the Editor, *The New Republic,* C (25 October 1939), 343.

7. Letter to the Editor, *The New Republic,* CII (15 January 1940), 88.

8. Letter to the Editor, *The New Republic,* CII (12 February 1940), 215.

9. Letter to the Editor, *The New Republic,* CII (29 April 1940), 579.

10. Letter to Random House on dust jacket of Budd Schulberg's *What Makes Sammy Run?* (New York: Random House, 1941).

11. Stanley Woodward's column, *New York Herald-Tribune* (8 January 1944), 13. Includes O'Hara letter.

12. Letter to the Editor, *New York Herald-Tribune* (7 March 1945), 22.

13. Red Smith's Column, *New York Herald-Tribune* (12 June 1952), 31. Includes O'Hara letter.

14. Letter to the Editor, *New York Herald-Tribune* (3 May 1957), 16.

15. Red Smith's Column, *New York Herald-Tribune* (31 August 1958), III, 1. Includes O'Hara letter.

16. Letter to Mark Schorer, 17 February 1959, *Sinclair Lewis An American Life* by Schorer (New York: McGraw-Hill, [1961], p. 351).

17. Letter to the Editor, *New York Herald-Tribune* (22 May 1959), 12.

18. Letter to the Editor, *New York Herald-Tribune* (5 April 1960), 18.

19. *The George and Ira Gershwin Song Book.* New York: Simon & Schuster, [1960]. O'Hara telegram, p. x.

20. Walter Farquhar, "Editorial Musings," *Pottsville Republican* (5 April 1961), 4. Includes O'Hara letter to Martin O'Hara.

21. Letter to the Editor, *New York Herald-Tribune* (20 August 1961), II, 3.

22. Letter to the Editor, *New York Times* (30 December 1961), 18.

23. Letter to the Editor, *New York Herald-Tribune* (26 January 1962), 16.

24. Letter to the Editor, *New York Herald-Tribune* (29 April 1962), II, 3.

25. Letter to the Editor, *New York Herald-Tribune* (5 June 1962), 20.

26. Letter to the Editor, *New York Herald-Tribune* (19 September 1962), 24.

27. Letter to the Editor, *New York Herald-Tribune* (28 September 1962), 24.

28. Letter to the Editor, *Yale Alumni Magazine*, XXVI November 1962), 7.

29. Red Smith's Column, *New York Herald-Tribune*—Paris Edition (18 January 1963), 9.

30. Letter to the Editor, *New York Herald-Tribune* (17 April 1963), 24.

31. Red Smith's Column, *New York Herald-Tribune* (28 January 1964), 20.

32. Red Smith's Column, *New York Herald-Tribune* (10 June 1964), 25.

33. "Dept. of Correction and Amplification," *The New Yorker*, XL (19 September 1964), 164–165.

34. Excerpts from Letters to Charles Poore, *Charles Hamilton Auction Number 56 . . . March 9, 1972* (item #226).

Book Reviews

‚‚

1. Review of *The Viking Portable Library Dorothy Parker,* *New York Times Book Review* (28 May 1944) , 5, 29.

2. Review of F. Scott Fitzgerald's *The Crack-Up,* *New York Times Book Review* (8 July 1945) , 3.

3. Review of Arthur Kober's *That Man Is Here Again, New York Times Book Review* (8 December 1946) , 7, 59.

4. Review of Eddie Condon's *We Called It Music, New York Times Book Review* (2 November 1947) , 6.

5. Review of Ernest Hemingway's *Across the River and Into the Trees, New York Times Book Review* (10 September 1950) , 1.

Verse

"Stars in My Eyes," *The New Yorker,* XV (6 May 1939) , 61.

"November March," Red Smith's Column, *New York Herald-Tribune* (6 November 1962) , 25.

Columns

»» »»»»

NEWSWEEK: "Entertainment Week" (15 July 1940–16 February 1942).

"An American in Memoriam," XVI (15 July 1940), 34.

"Into the Silences," XVI (22 July 1940), 36.

"The Theater's Annual Hay-Day," XVI (29 July 1940), 37.

"Hart Time," XVI (5 August 1940), 36.

"Pastor Hall—Not by Beethoven," XVI (12 August 1940), 41.

"Things to Come," XVI (19 August 1940), 44.

"Taking the Sleeper," XVI (26 August 1940), 50.

"Personal History," XVI (2 September 1940), 48.

"Heigh-ho, Wanger!" XVI (9 September 1940), 61.

"The Groaner," XVI (16 September 1940), 62.

"The Sun Shines East," XVI (23 September 1940), 50.

"You'll Have to Speak a Little Louder," XVI (30 September 1940), 58.

"With the Greatest of Ease," XVI (7 October 1940), 58.

"Yes, and No," XVI (14 October 1940), 74.

"Watch the O'Fearnas Go By," XVI (21 October 1940), 61.

"Charlie, Charley," XVI (28 October 1940), 60.

"100,000 Bucks County, Pa.," XVI (4 November 1940), 62.

"De Sylva Standard," XVI (11 November 1940), 60.

"Once Is a Lifetime," XVI (18 November 1940), 60.

"New York Is Calling," XVI (25 November 1940), 52.

"The Hayes Department," XVI (2 December 1940), 46.

" 'That's All There Is . . . ,' " XVI (9 December 1940), 64.

" 'Delicatessen Story,' " XVI (16 December 1940), 66.

"The Pace that Kills," XVI (23 December 1940), 50.

"Pshaw!" XVI (30 December 1940), 38.

"Christmas Presents," XVII (6 January 1941), 52.

"Rice to the West," XVII (13 January 1941), 52.

"Brewster Bodies," XVII (20 January 1941), 63.

"Whoopee and Stuff," XVII (27 January 1941), 46.

"Critic in the Dark," XVII (3 February 1941), 59.

"Valentine's Day Massacre," XVII (10 February 1941), 63.

"Have You Met Miss Jones?" XVII (17 February 1941), 67.

"All Wack and Some Play," XVII (24 February 1941), 60.

"What's On Your Mind?" XVII (3 March 1941), 60.

"A Claire," XVII (10 March 1941), 66.

" 'Citizen Kane,' " XVII (17 March 1941), 60.

"George Rx," XVII (24 March 1941), 70.

"The Coast is Clear," XVII (31 March 1941), 67.

"The Tables Down at Ciro's," XVII (7 April 1941), 62.

"Stumping the Expert," XVII (14 April 1941), 70.

"Bang, Bang, Bong," XVII (21 April 1941), 62.

"Prize Collection," XVII (28 April 1941), 64.

"Notes on Notes," XVII (5 May 1941), 66.

"All Packed?" XVII (12 May 1941), 62.

"Mutiny on a Bounty," XVII (19 May 1941), 76.

"Hallelujah," XVII (26 May 1941), 70.

"No Passports Required," XVII (2 June 1941), 52.

"What's Wrong?" XVII (9 June 1941), 60.

"Harvard: Fair," XVII (16 June 1941), 60.

"Chatter Column," XVII (23 June 1941), 54.

"Good Man in a Room," XVII (30 June 1941), 58.

"My Year," XVIII (7 July 1941), 52.

"Urgent!" XVIII (14 July 1941), 63.

"Thisa and Thata," XVIII (21 July 1941), 54.

"Conscientious Objector," XVIII (28 July 1941), 54.

"Hepburn or Snakes," XVIII (4 August 1941), 48.

"The Lady of 'The Lake,' " XVIII (11 August 1941), 62.

"America, I Love You," XVIII (18 August 1941), 58.

"Vox, Possibly, Humana," XVIII (25 August 1941), 52.

"One Season Coming Up," XVIII (1 September 1941), 48.

"Tramp, Tramp, Tramp," XVIII (8 September 1941), 70.

"Ahm a Poller," XVIII (15 September 1941), 54.

"Win With Wookey," XVIII (22 September 1941), 52.

"Boo!" XVIII (29 September 1941), 54.

"Senators vs. Dodgers," XVIII (6 October 1941), 58.

"The Children's Hour," XVIII (13 October 1941), 68.

"Complaint Department," XVIII (20 October 1941), 74.

"Grab-Bag," XVIII (27 October 1941), 60.

"Cool for 'Candle,' " XVIII (3 November 1941), 58.

"Show Enough," XVIII (10 November 1941), 70.

"Out of This World," XVIII (17 November 1941), 57.

"Hold, Enough!" XVIII (24 November 1941), 74.

"Hit and Misses," XVIII (1 December 1941), 71.

"Stage Wait," XVIII (8 December 1941), 68.

"What's New," XVIII (15 December 1941), 72.

"Broadway, Too," XVIII (22 December 1941), 61.

"Introduction to Tosca," XVIII (29 December 1941), 42.

"The Mantle of Mantle," XIX (5 January 1942), 55.

"Desire Under the Rose," XIX (12 January 1942), 46.

"N. Y. to L. A.," XIX (19 January 1942), 58.

"You're Like a Sweetheart of Mine," XIX (26 January 1942), 64.

"Report to the Nation," XIX (2 February 1942), 60.

"Harvard List," XIX (9 February 1942), 63.

"Is Evvabody Happy?" XIX (16 February 1942), 74.

TRENTON SUNDAY TIMES-ADVERTISER: "Sweet and Sour" (27 December 1953–27 June 1954).

27 December 1953, Part 4, p. 10; 3 January 1954, Part 4, p. 12; 10 January 1954, Part 4, p. 12; 17 January 1954, Part 4, p. 12; 24 January 1954, Part 4, p. 10; 31 January 1954, Part 4, p. 12; 7 February 1954, Part 4, p. 12; 14 February 1954, Part 4, p. 12; 21 February 1954, Part 4, p. 12; 28 February 1954, Part 4, p. 12; 7 March 1954, Part 4, p. 12;

14 March 1954, Part 4, p. 12; 21 March 1954, Part 4, p. 12; 28 March 1954, Part 4, p. 12; 4 April 1954, Part 4, p. 12; 11 April 1954, Part 4, p. 12; 18 April 1954, Part 4, p. 12; 25 April 1954, Part 4, p. 14; 2 May 1954, Part 4, p. 12; 9 May 1954, Part 4, p. 12; 16 May 1954, Part 4, p. 12; 23 May 1954, Part 4, p. 12; 30 May 1954, Part 4, p. 10; 6 June 1954, Part 4, p. 12; 13 June 1954, Part 4, p. 12; 20 June 1954, Part 4, p. 16; 27 June 1954, Part 4, p. 10.

COLLIER'S: "**Appointment With O'Hara**" (**5 February 1954–28 September 1956**).

CXXXIII: (5 February 1954), 6, 8; (19 February 1954), 6, 8; (5 March 1954), 16; (19 March 1954), 6, 8; (2 April 1954), 6; (16 April 1954), 6, 8; (30 April 1954), 6, 8; (14 May 1954), 6, 8; (28 May 1954), 6, 8; (11 June 1954), 6; (25 June 1954), 6, 8.

CXXXIV: (9 July 1954), 6, 8; (23 July 1954), 6; (6 August 1954), 6; (20 August 1954), 6; (3 September 1954), 6; (17 September 1954), 6, 8; (1 October 1954), 6, 8; (15 October 1954), 6, 8; (29 October 1954), 6, 8; (12 November 1954), 6, 8; (26 November 1954), 6, 8; (10 December 1954), 6, 8; (24 December 1954), 6, 8.

CXXXV: (7 January 1955), 12–13; (21 January 1955), 6, 8; (4 February 1955), 6, 8; (18 February 1955), 6; (4 March 1955), 6; (18 March 1955), 6, 8; (1 April 1955), 6, 8; (15 April 1955), 6, 8; (29 April 1955), 6, 8; (13 May 1955), 6, 8; (27 May 1955), 6, 8; (10 June 1955), 6, 8; (24 June 1955), 6, 8.

CXXXVI: (8 July 1955), 6, 8; (22 July 1955), 6, 8; (5 August 1955), 6–7; (19 August 1955), 6, 8; (2 September 1955),

6; (16 September 1955), 6, 8; (30 September 1955), 6, 8; (14 October 1955), 6, 8; (28 October 1955), 6, 8; (9 December 1955), 6, 8; (23 December 1955), 6, 8.

CXXXVII: (6 January 1956), 6; (20 January 1956), 8; (3 February 1956), 6, 8; (17 February 1956), 6; (2 March 1956), 6; (16 March 1956), 6, 8; (30 March 1956), 6, 8; (13 April 1956), 6, 8; (27 April 1956), 6; (11 May 1956), 6; (25 May 1956), 6, 8; (8 June 1956), 8; (22 June 1956), 6, 8.

CXXXVIII: (6 July 1956), 6, 8; (20 July 1956), 6; (3 August 1956), 6; (17 August 1956), 6; (31 August 1956), 6; (14 September 1956), 6; (28 September 1956), 6.

NEWSDAY: "My Turn" (3 October 1964–2 October 1965)— Syndicated.

3 October 1964, 4W; 10 October 1964, 4W; 17 October 1964, 4W; 24 October 1964, 4W; 31 October 1964, 4W; 7 November 1964, 4W; 14 November 1964, 4W; 21 November 1964, 4W; 28 November 1964, 4W; 5 December 1964, 4W; 12 December 1964, 4W; 19 December 1964, 4W; 26 December 1964, 4W; 2 January 1965, 4W; 9 January 1965, 4W; 16 January 1965, 4W; 23 January 1965, 4W; 30 January 1965, 4W; 6 February 1965, 4W; 13 February 1965, 4W; 29 February 1965, 4W; 27 February 1965, 4W; 6 March 1965, 4W; 13 March 1965, 4W; 20 March 1965, 4W; 27 March 1965, 4W; 3 April 1965, 4W; 10 April 1965, 4W; 17 April 1965, 4W; 24 April 1965, 4W; 1 May 1965, 4W; 8 May 1965, 4W; 15 May 1965, 4W; 22 May 1965, 4W; 29 May 1965, 4W; 5 June 1965, 4W; 12 June 1965, 4W; 19 June 1965, 4W; 26 June 1965, 4W; 3 July 1965, 4W; 10 July 1965, 4W; 17 July 1965, 4W; 24 July 1965, 4W; 31 July 1965, 6W; 7 August 1965,

4W; 14 August 1965, 4W; 21 August 1965, 4W; 28 August 1965, 4W; 4 September 1965, 4W; 11 September 1965, 4W; 18 September 1965, 4W; 25 September 1965, 4W; 2 October 1965, 4W.

Collected in *My Turn.*

HOLIDAY: "The Whistle Stop" (September 1966–May 1967).

"Eunuchs in the Harem," XL (September 1966), 16, 20–21.

"Egos and Actors," XL (October 1966), 34, 37–38.

"Put Up Your Dukes," XL (November 1966), 20, 24–25.

"The Error of Our Ways," XL (December 1966), 22, 24, 27.

"Reflections of a Non-Travel Writer," XLI (January 1967), 24, 26, 28–29.

"The Follies of Broadway," XLI (February 1967), 23, 25.

"A Harvest of Sour Grapes," XLI (March 1967), 20, 24, 26.

"When Big Bands Were Big," XLI (April 1967), 20, 23, 26.

"If the Name Fits," XLI (May 1967), 28, 30–31.

Appendix: Compiler's Notes

»»»

1. *Journalism*
   1924–1926 Reporter for the *Pottsville Journal.* No file of the paper for these years has been located.
   1927 Reporter for the *Tamaqua Courier,* January–March. No by-line.
   1928–1933 Reporter for the *New York Herald-Tribune;* rewrite man for the *New York Daily Mirror;* radio columnist for the *New York Morning Telegraph* (by-line—Franey Delaney); reporter for *Time* (August 1928–March 1929); reporter for *Editor & Publisher;* managing editor of the *Pittsburgh Bulletin Index* (see below).

2. *Pittsburgh Bulletin Index*
   O'Hara's work was not by-lined, but former staffers have attributed the following to him:

   "Joe: Straight Man" (18 May 1933), 4, 12.
   "Polo" (27 July 1933), 6–7.
   Reply to letter (17 August 1933), 15. Underground travel in New York City.

3. *The Conning Tower*
   In the twenties and thirties O'Hara contributed items to Franklin P. Adams' column, "The Conning Tower," in the *New York World* and the *New York Herald-Tribune;* only one (*Herald-Tribune,* 10 July 1931, 20) has so far been identified.

4. *Spiral-Bound Advance Proofs*
   The following spiral-bound advance proofs from Random House have been seen by the compiler:

   Ourselves to Know (1960)
   Sermons and Soda-Water (1960)
   The Lockwood Concern (1965)
   Waiting for Winter (1966)

And Other Stories (1968)
Lovey Childs (1969)

There were almost certainly others.

5. *Blurbs*
   The following specially written statements have been noted. Excerpts from O'Hara's writings used as blurbs have been omitted.

   Budd Schulberg, *What Makes Sammy Run?* (New York: Random House, 1941) . See Letters section.
   Charles Mercer, *The Reckoning* (New York: Dell, [1963]) . Statement on front cover.
   John K. Hutchens, *One Man's Montana* (Philadelphia & New York: Lippincott, 1964) . Statement on dust jacket.

6. *Hollywood Credits*
   O'Hara received screen credit for the following motion-picture scripts:

   I Was an Adventuress (Fox, 1940)
   He Married His Wife (Fox, 1940)
   Moontide (Fox, 1942)
   The Best Things in Life Are Free (Fox, 1956)

7. *Unlocated Clipping*
   "Good Reading," c. 1934. O'Hara recommends 6 books: *Man's Fate, Tender is the Night, A Farewell to Arms, Laments for the Living, The Last Adam, The Great Gatsby.*

8. *The New Yorker*
   O'Hara's unsigned contributions to "The Talk of the Town" and other departments cannot be identified.

MATTHEW J. BRUCCOLI, Professor of English at the University of South Carolina, has written or edited some thirty books on American literature. He is Director of the Center for Editions of American Authors and edits the *Fitzgerald/Hemingway Annual*. He is now working on a biography of John O'Hara.

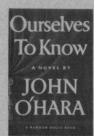

Ourselves To Know
A NOVEL BY
JOHN O'HARA
A RANDOM HOUSE BOOK

THE CAPE COD LIGHTER
A COLLECTION OF 23 NEW STORIES BY
JOHN O'HARA
A RANDOM HOUSE BOOK

MY TURN
fifty-three pieces by **John O'Hara**
A Random House Book

Hellbox
BY JOHN O'HARA
A RANDOM HOUSE BOOK

PAL JOEY
BY
John O'Hara

A
FAMILY PARTY
JOHN O'HARA

PIPE NIGHT
JOHN O'HARA

ASSEMBLY
A COLLECTION OF 26 NEW STORIES BY
JOHN O'HARA
A RANDOM HOUSE BOOK

John O'Hara The Evrings
A NOVEL

JOHN O'HARA
Five Plays
The Farmers Hotel
The Searching Sun
The Champagne Pool
Veronique
The Way It Was
With a Foreword by the Author

JOHN O'HARA
The Instrument

THE HORSE KNOWS THE WAY
A COLLECTION OF 28 NEW STORIES BY
JOHN O'HARA
A RANDOM HOUSE BOOK

John O'Hara The Time Element & Other Stories
34 previously uncollected stories

SERMONS AND SODA-WATER
JOHN O'HARA

AND OTHER STORIES
A COLLECTION OF 12 NEW STORIES BY
JOHN O'HARA
A RANDOM HOUSE BOOK

ELIZABETH APPLETON
A NOVEL BY
JOHN O'HARA
A RANDOM HOUSE BOOK